Also by Charles Handy

The New Philanthropists (with Elizabeth Handy)
Myself and Other More Important Matters
Reinvented Lives (with Elizabeth Handy)
The Elephant and the Flea
Thoughts for the Day (previously published as *Waiting
for the Mountain to Move*)
The New Alchemists (with Elizabeth Handy)
The Hungry Spirit
Beyond Certainty
The Empty Raincoat
Inside Organizations
The Age of Unreason
Understanding Voluntary Organizations
Understanding Schools as Organizations
The Future of Work
Gods of Management
Understanding Organizations

THE SECOND CURVE

Charles Handy

THE SECOND CURVE

Thoughts on Reinventing Society

BOOKS

1 3 5 7 9 10 8 6 4 2

Random House Books
20 Vauxhall Bridge Road
London SW1V 2SA

Random House Books is part of the Penguin Random House group of
companies whose addresses can be found at global.penguinrandomhouse.com.

Penguin
Random House
UK

First published by Random House Books in 2015

www.randomhouse.co.uk

A CIP catalogue record for this book is available from the British Library.

ISBN: 9781847941329 (Hardback)
ISBN: 9781847941336 (Trade Paperback)

Typeset in Adobe Garamond 12.5/15 pt by
Palimpsest Book Production Limited, Falkirk, Stirlingshire

Printed and bound by Clays Ltd, St Ives plc

Penguin Random House is committed to a sustainable future for our
business, our readers and our planet. This book is made from Forest
Stewardship Council® certified paper.

To my grandchildren
Leo, Sam, Nephele, Scarlett
who will have to live and work in the world
I am envisaging.

CONTENTS

ACKNOWLEDGEMENTS

MANY PEOPLE, OFTEN unknowingly, have contributed to this book. It was Gail Rebuck, my long-time publisher, friend and adviser, who suggested that I might revisit some of my ideas from two decades back to see whether they still applied in today's circumstances. This tempted me not only to revisit those ideas but to spread my wings a bit wider and push the idea of the Second Curve into other areas of society beyond those of the organisation. Nigel Wilcockson, my editor at Random House, then helped to shape these ideas into a book. I am grateful to him for his patience and gentle persuasion as I struggled to find a way to structure my thoughts, while Rosalind Fergusson corrected my erring facts and my verbal infelicities with great tact.

Many are those who have influenced my thinking down the years. I am thinking of the now-departed great gurus of management, Warren Bennis (my old friend and mentor) and Peter Drucker. Jim O'Toole, Aristotelian interpreter, and Michael Maccoby, whose psychoanalytical and anthropological background provided new insights into leadership, have also been among my informal teachers down the years. Then there are all those scholars whose books fill my shelves and whose ideas have rubbed off on me down the years, in particular Tom Peters, Jim Collins, Lynda Gratton, Mark Goyder and John Kay, although they should not be held responsible for anything I have written here.

Richard Straub, founder of the Drucker Forum in Vienna, has been a constant source of support and inspiration, while journalists such as Simon Caulkin and Adrian Wooldridge have fed my head with their stimulating articles and ideas. Then there is Gordon Fox; Buddhist, philosopher, businessman and inspiring friend who has shown me how good principles can build great businesses. I am indebted to all these wise folk and to many others too numerous to list.

The book, however, would never have happened without my wife and partner, Elizabeth. Her unwavering belief in me has eclipsed my doubts, her good sense has restrained my wilder excesses, while her unfailing support and affection has underpinned my life.

INTRODUCTION

Why did I write this book?
Who would I like to read it?

'SIGN HERE, PLEASE,' the man said, 'and put the date, but be sure you write the year in full. We can get confused between the centuries here.' He was the clerk of works at Windsor Castle and had just handed me an ancient key that went with my new job. I smiled at what I thought was a joke but when I looked up he was obviously serious. I should have been warned.

I was there to be Warden, an appropriately Trollopian title I later felt, of a Study and Conference Centre focusing on the ethical and value issues that would face individuals and society in the future. I was fascinated by the history of the castle. The house that we were given to live in had been built for the young Henry III in 1216. The whole place reeked of history. I had hoped to create a nest of creative thinking in this treasury of the past but I soon realised that history and tradition can be a prison as well as a thing to be treasured. I discovered that if something has been done that way for centuries it needs a looming disaster to allow any change from the status quo. There is some sense in that but it means that progress is slow, often a series of unplanned responses to emergencies rather than a planned pursuit of a vision. It was frustrating for this new arrival who wanted to build on that history but felt stymied by the guardians of tradition.

Having left Windsor I realised that much of life, even outside the castle, was governed by the same principle of 'If it works don't fix it.' Exhortations that it won't work like that much longer, or could work better, fall on deaf ears. The status quo, people kept telling me, has to be better than the unknown. If there has to be change it should be 'better than yesterday', not different. But society is not working as it should. Living is getting harder, not easier, for most. Inequality is growing. Wealth is not trickling down as it used to do. Nor is it trickling up, as in theory it should do, because consumers are ensnared in debt, spending too much on their houses, with too little left over to fuel the economy with their spending. Too many of the customs, practices and institutions of society were designed for a time that has passed. The internet and its corollaries are revolutionising much of our lives, but taking the guts out of many of our institutions as they do so. The Western world seems to have gone into retirement mode, settling for a cautious life after the financial scares of the last decade, hoping that the comfortable life we had become used to will soon return if we only keep our nerve. The reality, however, is that we can neither bring back the past nor prolong the present indefinitely. When the world changes around us we have to change as well, or, as Tancredi famously told his uncle the Prince in Lampedusa's novel *The Leopard*, 'For things to remain the same, things will have to change.' Unfortunately, bold thinking has become suspect or too risky among those supposedly responsible for our future. Governments tweak and twist and adapt but are more concerned to stay in power than to conjure up new visions and new possibilities.

This is happening at a time when many of our assumptions about how our lives work are being turned upside down by new technologies and new values. Forget for a moment the big dramas of international affairs, it is our daily lives that are going to change the most. This book is dedicated to my young grand-children who will grow into a world very different from the one that I encountered but who are being prepared for it as if nothing will be very different from the world that I knew, that there will be jobs for them if they put their heads down and pass their exams, jobs and exams not that different from the ones I encountered 60 or more years ago. That is a recipe for disappoint-ment and disillusion. For one thing, half of today's jobs will already be gone by 2030, forecasters say, but how then do you prepare young people for a world that does not yet exist and cannot be foreseen?

I confess that I have little idea how my grand-children or their contemporaries will be earning their living 30 years from now, how society will be organised around them as more and more of life happens virtually, whether the nation state will still rule their lives or will have been replaced by city states and confederations, how they will measure success in their lives or how they will choose to live. Anything that is based on information, be it books, music or entertainment, will effectively be free, but a world of free goods offers few paying jobs. If they do find or, better, create any work that pays they will need to keep doing it well into their eighties so they had better enjoy it.

Those young people are already living in a world dominated by information at their fingertips and contacts at the press of a button or just the sound of their voice. This technology can only get faster, better and easier to use, but with consequences that are hard to foresee. Will the new technology make their lives simpler or more confusing? Where will they hide, if they need to, when too much information or too much communication becomes uncomfortable? Will the flow of information tempt them to become indecisive and reactive because it is too easy to delay decisions until you know more, and there always could be more, or to fill your time responding to the incoming messages on whatever gadget sits in your hand, with no time left over for original thought or action? Can you rely on friends or colleagues that you only meet virtually? Will algorithms rule our lives, with formulae and programs for every eventuality? The uncertainties thrown up by the new media are worrying but technological change often produces more questions than solutions.

Already, as I see it, too much of all that is new favours the few and not the many. Society is out of balance. Power is unequally distributed. In business, the information economy is turning into a winner-takes-all one, where the likes of Amazon, Facebook and Google dominate and gobble up any daring newcomer. We need to challenge orthodoxy, dream a little, think unreasonably and dare the impossible if we are going to have any chance of making the future work for all of us, not just those favoured few. That was the origin of the thinking behind the principle of the Second Curve, the key strand of this book.

The message of the Second Curve is that to move forward in many areas of life it is sometimes necessary to change radically, to start a new course that will be different from the existing one, often requiring a whole new way of looking at familiar problems, what Thomas Kuhn called a paradigm shift. I explain the idea more fully in the first essay. The real problem is that the change has to be initiated while the first curve is still going. That means that those who have been in charge of that first curve have to begin to think very differently about the future, or, more often, let others lead the way up the new curve. That is something that does not come easily. Why change when all is well, we ask ourselves. Change is easier to envisage when crisis looms but harder to implement with resources and time running out.

The good news for the Second Curve is that, despite the recent upheavals in some parts of the world, things have been going well for the great majority of people over the last half-century. If we compare life now with life as it was then, the human race is healthier and wealthier, and lives longer and better, than ever before in history. The average person everywhere earns three times as much as they did 50 years ago and the array of things that they can buy with that money would amaze my parents' generation were they alive to witness it. A speaker at a recent conference in the hills of the Tyrol wondered why anyone there would want to live anywhere other than Europe today, despite all its internal wranglings. What this means, according to the theory of the Second Curve, is that these are now the perfect conditions for rethinking the ways in which we run society, for making the most of the abundance that we have created for ourselves. Complacency is a sign of looming danger but also of opportunity. Doing nothing risks losing what you have.

In the essays that follow I try to apply the idea of the Second Curve to a range of issues, from capitalism and government to education and the definition of the good life, with much in between. There is no ideology behind my thinking other than the philosophy of that Second Curve, that we urgently need new directions in all the arenas of life. One very clear new curve emerged as I wrote, namely the need for an increasing emphasis on self-responsibility. My grandchildren and their like are going to be on their own out there, much more so than I was. We can no longer rely on the institutions of education and the workplace to prepare us for life and look after us during it. It was too easy in the past to let others direct our life. I passed from school to university to business or profession. In each I was told what to do and how to do it. That will no longer happen and if it does the directions may well be wrong. There will inevitably be less loyalty to those institutions. They will care less for us and we for them. That is because most contracts will have to be more temporary, partly because the institutions themselves will be less permanent, and our stay in them more fleeting. Our communities will be those of shared interest rather than of a common place or institution. Communities of interest are more fun and more collegial but feel less responsible for their members' other lives. Outside the community everyone must fend for themselves. Relationships and marriages today sometimes seem more like communities of interest than of shared responsibility, so that when the common interests die so does the relationship. When insecurity is rife, each must make their own safe harbour. Life won't be easy.

I have not delved into the arena of national party politics, nor will I be discussing wider and bigger issues such as climate change, the future of the European

Union, the rise of China and the schisms within Islam. These are clearly important matters that will have an impact on the lives of future generations, but as individuals we can have only limited influence, if any, on their outcomes. More honestly, I have to recognise that the topics are beyond my area of competence. Like everyone else, I have my opinions but they are worth no more than those of anyone else. I could say, for example, that the real challenge of climate change lies in making the right adjustments to what is already irreversible, even if we can perhaps slow down the rate of change. I could predict that most of us will end up living in air-conditioned cities, rather like Singapore, and grow to like it, as I did when I lived there. But I know more knowledgeable experts who tell me that I am too pessimistic and they may be right. I could predict that Europe will end up with an inner federation of the original six countries and an outer ring made up of a confederation of nation states, but, again, I could be wrong. I could predict that China will eventually go federal with a strong but small centre and many autonomous regions, but even if I were right there is little that I could do about it other than to observe. For Islam I can only watch, worry and reflect that when religion becomes tribal it can go viral. Leaving these big issues aside, there are challenges enough in the things that we can usefully influence in some way.

The book therefore is a collection of essays on these challenges, short pieces too, because in years gone by

INTRODUCTION

I regularly wrote and broadcast a Thought for the Day
on the BBC's morning radio programme *Today*. I learnt
much from writing those Thoughts. I learnt, for
instance, that brevity focuses the mind, of both the
listener and the author. We were allowed no more than
450 words – two minutes and forty-five seconds. It
wasn't easy. I always wanted more time, more words,
but those Thoughts were perfectly adapted to the bite-
sized world that we all now live in. Radio may allow
an uninterrupted two and a bit minutes, but television
wants a new image every 20 seconds and tweeters have
to make do with 140 characters.

I now read executive summaries of essays and
reports and only dip into the main body if I have to.
My study is piled high with books that I have bought
with the idea of reading them diligently and thoroughly
until the day comes when I know that I won't. I add
them to my overflowing bookshelves which are now
more truthfully a visual display of good intentions.
Instead I read reviews of new books in the Sunday
papers and kid myself that I need not then buy the
actual book, or read it if I do. I used to plan my own
books to be short enough to be read on a plane flight
from London to Los Angeles, believing that only then
would any of my likely readers actually have the
requisite amount of uninterrupted time. But now, with
on-board telephones and the ever-present BlackBerry
or iPhone, even those quiet periods have been curtailed.

So my books have to get shorter, or, at least, the

individual chapters have to be cut down to size if I want busy people to read them. I have been generous and allowed myself around 3,000 words for each essay in this book. There are 16 of them in total, short for a book but enough, I hope, to make one pause and reflect. Being short, they have to avoid the detail in order to concentrate on the principles at stake. That is both their defect and their advantage. They draw on my own experience of life as much as on research, which makes them more personal than authoritative, but, perhaps, more interesting as a result. That stories help was something else that I learnt from those Thoughts for the Day, stories that illustrate the message, modern parables.

I claim no special expertise. I think of myself as a social philosopher and philosophers tend to pose questions rather than provide precise answers. It is not, therefore, a prescriptive book. I do not pretend to know what the Second Curve should be in each scenario, although I offer some provocative suggestions, intended more as invitations to my readers to think beyond the familiar. Sometimes even the questions, let alone the answers, are too important to be left to the experts, who tend to look at the trees rather than the wood, missing the big changes that are looming while they concentrate on the particulars. Some of the essays, I realise, may be of more immediate interest than others. It is not, therefore, a book to be necessarily read straight through from cover to cover, but to be savoured more à la carte, depending on your interests at the time. Those who are familiar with my earlier writings may notice some ideas and metaphors reappearing here and there, including the concept of the Second Curve itself. These low-definition concepts worked for me then, 25 years ago, and reconfigured for a different world they still, I hope, illuminate some of our dilemmas.

Looking back now, after eight decades of life, I wonder how it was that, for the first three decades at least, I seldom questioned the way things worked, or were supposed to work, in Britain and in much of the rest of the world. I assumed that because things had always been that way that was the way they were meant to be; that those in authority knew what they were doing and were well advised. I know better now. Although I am hugely impressed with most of the teenagers whom I meet, I doubt that they are much better informed than I was about the world that lies ahead of them or the very real dilemmas that they will face in deciding how to live their lives. I would like to encourage them to challenge the status quo whenever they meet it, to question conventional wisdom and to be bold in shaping their own lives. That said, I would urge their elders to do likewise if they can stand back from their busy lives to see where they are heading.

One of the purposes of the Windsor centre of which I was warden was to bring together, over a weekend, some of the opinion-formers of the nation, those at the top of the professions, of business, politics and the armed forces. The intention was to help them to focus on the big ethical and moral issues facing society. The discussions were fascinating and the people interesting but I found that they were more anxious to expound their own ideas than to listen to those of the others, let alone to change their own minds. There was no thought of Second Curves in those meetings. We therefore decided to add another set of discussions, this time inviting the rising stars of the next generation. These people had no declared positions that they needed to defend; they were more willing to listen and to contemplate alternative views. The scenarios they came up with were more exciting, at least to me. The hope was that they would recall these conversations when they in their turn were in a position to influence events.

That may have been too optimistic. The pace of change in a democracy is glacial, to be measured in generations not years. Governments may often know what they should do, but not how to get re-elected after doing it. Some of the suggestions offered in the course of the Windsor discussions and many of my own proposals in this book would need a dictatorship to bring them about, or at least a new generation impatient for change and long primed with ideas of what that change should be. Democratic governments can only move when they know that the move will be widely accepted. As a result the directions of change often come from outside the parliamentary system, not from within it; from people like us, in short.

It is, therefore, to the next generation that this book is addressed. My hope is that the book will kindle their curiosity, provoke and stir their imagination, and encourage discussion among friends and colleagues. It was John Maynard Keynes who said, 'I am sure that the power of vested interests is vastly exaggerated compared with the gradual encroachment of ideas.' David Hume had earlier said that truth proceeds from argument among friends. I agree with both of them. My best delight is to debate with friends of a evening around a supper table, well supplied with wine. We can change our world by talking, to each other. If this short book can provide the stimulus for more of those conversations I shall be well satisfied. My aim, however, is to stimulate not to prescribe for I know only too well that the devil is in the detail, and that others will know the details better than I.

THE ESSAYS

1

THE SECOND CURVE

What is it? How do we find it?

THINKING ABOUT IT, I must have been a very irritating husband, in more ways than one, no doubt, but principally because I kept changing my job just when things were going well. After ten years with Shell I had reached the small country manager stage, the first step to greater things, when I decided that the life of an oil executive was not for me, that I would rather teach managers than be one. The old saying 'if you can't do it, teach it' probably applied, if I am honest. To Shell's surprise, and even perhaps disappointment, I turned down the posting and resigned.

After two years of readjusting and retraining I joined the London Business School: six years later I reached the exalted rank of a full professor with my first book published and the holy grail of tenure (guaranteed employment until retirement) granted, only to decide that it was not what I wanted to spend my life doing. That was to be a full-time writer. It took four years in one more job to build up the courage to cut that umbilical cord that ties one to the womb of an organisation. Only then did I feel that I had come into my own. Just in time, too, or I would have ended up in Davy's Bar.

I have often, down the years, told my story of the road to Davy's Bar, and its imagery, along with its implications, still haunts me. This is the story as it happened then, for Davy's Bar is no longer there: I was driving through the Wicklow Mountains, the bare but beautiful hills outside Dublin, when I lost my way. I saw a man walking his dog so I stopped beside him and asked if he could point me on the way to Avoca, where I was heading. 'Surely,' he said, 'and it's dead easy. You go straight ahead up this hill then down again for a mile or so until you get to a stream with a bridge over it; on the other side of it you'll see Davy's Bar; you can't miss it, it is very bright red. Have you got that now?' 'I think so,' I said. 'Straight up, then down, until I come to Davy's Bar.' 'Great; well, half a mile before you get there, turn right up the hill and that will take you to Avoca.'

I had thanked him and driven off before I realised the strange Irish logic of his directions. But its message stuck with me until I started talking about the challenge of the Second Curve, that turn to the right up the hill which you will often have passed without knowing it was where you should have gone. I have met too many organisations (and, indeed, individuals) parked in the equivalent of Davy's Bar, having realised, too late, that they have missed the turn to the future and can only look back regretfully and drown their sadness with a mournful drink or two, while they reminisce about the good times and what might have been.

Unwittingly, in my career, I was riding a sequence of roads up the hill, having turned each time before I got to the equivalent of Davy's Bar. When I drew the curves out, my up-and-down trajectory began to make sense. Since then the curves have influenced much of my thinking about change and, more generally, the future. The idea of the sigmoid curves, as they are properly called, is a metaphor. Metaphors are a great aid to understanding, not to be dismissed because they are not strictly scientific. They are low-definition concepts, imprecise in detail but unexpectedly revealing in the way we look at things. There will be many more of them in this book.

The sigmoid curve is an S-shaped curve on its side, like this:

The sigmoid curve is a mathematical concept. Used as a metaphor it is a familiar idea to many. The phrases 'learning curve' and 'ahead of the curve' refer to it and many businesses use it when projecting the future. What is not always realised, however, is that it is much more than that. It is the line of all things human, of our own lives, of organisations and businesses, of governments, empires and alliances, of democracy itself and its many and varied institutions. In each case there is, or was, an initial period of investment – be it financial, of education (in the case of our own lives) or of trial and experiment – a period when the input exceeds the output, when the line of the S dips down. More goes out than comes in. Then, as results begin to show and glimmers of progress emerge, the line moves up. If all goes well it continues to rise, but the time comes when, inevitably, the curve peaks and begins its descent. The descent can be prolonged, and often is, but oblivion waits at the end.

There seems to be no escape from the sigmoid curve. The only variable is the length of the curve. The Roman Empire lasted 400 years, but finally reached its end. Other empires lasted less long before they dipped, as the British Empire did and the American one surely will. Governments and dictatorships ultimately outstay their welcome. On a smaller scale, businesses used to last on average for 40 years before they collapsed or were taken over; now the average lifespan appears to have dropped to a mere 14 years. The speed of the curve seems to be accelerating although we humans seem to have stretched out our own personal curves to 90 years or more. There is, however, still oblivion of some sort at the end. It could be a depressing prospect.

But it need not be. There can always be a Second Curve, like this:

Obvious, you might think, but there is a problem. The nasty and often fatal snag is that the Second Curve has to start before the first curve peaks. Only then are there enough resources – of money, time and energy – to cover that first initial dip, the investment period. If you try to draw the Second Curve as one taking off after the peak, when that first curve is turning down, it doesn't work, on paper or in reality; the Second Curve never gets up high enough unless you give it a sharp kink. The problem, however, is knowing when that first line is about to peak. Psychologically, when everything is going well it is reasonable to expect it to continue, other things being equal. Why not project the present into the future when it is so obviously successful? Success, however, puts blinkers on us, discourages doubt, re-inforces itself. Only in retrospect can we look back and say, 'That was it, that was the peak, that was when we should have started to think anew.' Unfortunately, being wise after the event is too late to be useful.

First-curve success can blind one to the possibilities of a new technology or a new market, allowing others to seize the initiative. Clayton Christensen of Harvard Business School termed it the problem of disruptive innovation, citing, among many others, the case of Kodak, who ignored the possibilities of digital photography until it was too late. They allowed outsiders to intrude and, in my words, create the new curve instead of them. New technology is offering the chance of those new curves every day. Spotting them and seizing them is the new strategic challenge for education, health and government as well as business.

Yet when your income, productivity or reputation is falling it is hard to contemplate anything new. Anyone who has experienced unemployment will remember how hard it was to summon up the confidence or the energy, let alone the wherewithal, to make an investment in something potentially risky. Governments find this as hard as individuals, which is why the Keynesian advice to invest your way out of recession is intuitively so difficult to act on. When money is short it is counter-intuitive to spend more. Second-Curve thinking comes hard when times are hard. In business it may mean competing with yourself, even cannibalising your existing product. Do it instead when times are good; before the downturn.

Some institutions, and some people, do struggle up to the second line from a descending curve but only with tremendous effort and great sacrifice, in order to generate what is needed to cover that initial dip in the curve. For organisations it means taking a knife to the headcount and the overheads, regrouping the organisation, which often involves the replacement of the top management, and, most painful of all, discarding some cherished products and markets. In practice this only happens when the concern is taken over by another business with fewer qualms about the necessary surgery. Private-equity firms could justify their reshaping of the businesses that they buy by arguing that only in that way can the businesses find their Second Curve.

Looking back over my career I had, without realising it, done the right thing at the right time. Each time I had left my job before it peaked. My new curve then dipped down, financially, for some years while I invested in new learning until the new curve took off, only for it, in time, to approach its peak. A further curve, I suspect, is yet to come. Many will have had a similar experience in their own lives, moving from one job to another, unwittingly riding the sigmoid curves, but Second-Curve thinking goes far beyond personal careers.

Steve Jobs of Apple was, by all accounts, a difficult man to work with, but he was the master of the Second Curve. By the time that the Macintosh computer was a proven success Jobs and his creative team were already planning to enter the music business with the iPod. When that product began to dominate the market Jobs had already begun to design the iPhone, a new product for a very different business, that was followed, once successful, by the iPad. Each new curve was conceived before the last one peaked. Each new curve grew out of the last but sold into a very different market – on the face of it, a dangerous risk but to Jobs a logical next curve. Today the Apple products seem to be a seamless interconnected family, but that was neither inevitable nor predictable. Will Second-Curve thinking continue at Apple? Time will tell, because Second-Curve thinking does not come easily. It requires imagination, intuition and instinct more than rational analysis. Then, to act on it demands the courage to step into the unknown when all the signals, and all those around you, tell you that you don't need to.

In another realm and another game, Alex Ferguson, the legendary manager of Manchester United Football Club, was careful to bring on new talent before the current top players passed their peak, even though that meant occasionally losing stars who still had some playing time in them. It is, unfortunately, always going to be difficult to keep the creators of the first curve engaged while building the future beneath them. The obvious answer is to help them to create the beginnings of a Second Curve for themselves, but not until your own Second Curve has been established. Timing is all. A large part of Alex Ferguson's prolonged success was due to getting the Second-Curve timing right. He could not have raised the club to the top of the football world and kept it there for 27 years if he had not ridden the sigmoid curves, although, of course, he was not aware of the concept. Just as Molière's Monsieur Jourdain found that he had been speaking prose for 40 years without knowing it, so many successful people have reinvented themselves or their organisations without the help of the idea. Sadly, in retrospect, Alex Ferguson failed at the end. He resigned when the club was already at its peak, leaving his successor to build a new curve when the first one had already started to decline. If Ferguson had gone two years earlier the club's momentum might have provided the time needed to build the credibility of the new leader and the chance to start the new curve.

Contrast these and my own examples with the story of a man I met at a local party. He was standing on his own, in the corner, while the party went on around him. Elderly, obviously, but also a bit lost, so I went over to talk to him. 'Have you lived here long?' I asked. 'Yes,' he replied, and added, 'I'm 93, you know,' although I had not asked. 'Is that so?' I said. 'Then you must have had a fascinating life – tell me about it.'

'Well, when the war broke out I was 19. I tried to join up but they said that my lungs weren't up to it and that I must do industrial work instead. They offered me the choice of two factories, one north of the Thames, one south. Since I lived north I chose that one. That was where I stayed for the next 40 years, moving up a couple of levels during that time. Then I retired and came to live here.'

'And then. . . ? I prompted him. 'That's it,' he said. Then, after a long pause, he added, 'Sometimes

I think that I should have done something more with my life.'

A moderately successful life followed by a long slow decline into eventual oblivion. Nothing wrong with that, I mused, except for what might have been. Why was it such a familiar story? Why did it remind me irresistibly of so many people whom I knew, with long years spent compiling a CV that now seemed irrelevant, of so many businesses and other institutions, indeed of much of the country where I was living, many parts of which, it seemed to me, had failed to find the best road to a different future and had settled instead for making the best of what was there, walking backwards into the future, clinging as long as possible to what used to be, ending up with a long drink at Davy's Bar while reminiscing about the past.

It is perhaps no wonder that Second-Curve thinking and action is rarer than it should be, in our own lives or in the lives of institutions. Sometimes a trigger is required. Businesses can sense from the shrinking of profit margins or market shares that new thinking is needed. Athletes know that age imposes its own limits, often at an unfairly early stage, and that a new career has to be planned while success still keeps your name in the news. The manager of Wigan rugby league club once told me that his biggest problem was to convince a strapping 25-year-old athlete at the height of his powers that he needed to start re-educating himself for another way of life in three or four years' time.

Retirement, redundancy or divorce can be the trigger for some individuals, although leaving it until it happens can be leaving it too late. Sometimes it is the boredom that can come from success. Been there, done that. André Previn, the classical musician, had great success in Hollywood as a young man, composing film scores, but gave it all up to come to Britain and concentrate on performing and conducting. He explained that he woke up one morning with no pain in his stomach at the thought of what he had to do that day. At that point, he knew it was time to leave.

The threat of a takeover can be the trigger for a business. A period in opposition is the equivalent of a sabbatical for politicians and should be an invitation to a bout of Second-Curve thinking. Anything that takes us out of our comfort zones for a while can act as a reminder that the past we are used to may not be our best future. Sabbaticals for senior executives, or temporary secondments to a different world, ought to be more common than they are. As Dr Johnson once said, you can see your own country much more clearly when you stand outside it. Institutions, in particular, are notoriously unwilling to die, seeing it as their duty to soldier on against the odds. Jim Collins, the American management scholar and writer, has usefully listed the five stages of institutional decline down that slippery slope of the first curve, what Christensen called the technological mudslide. First there is the hubris born of success, at the top of the curve, then the undisciplined pursuit of more of the same, followed by a denial of any risk. Thereafter there is only a futile grasping for salvation and an eventual capitulation to irrelevance or death. It is sadly fascinating to watch too many institutions following Jim Collins' slow progression, usually by trying to do more of the same only cheaper, leaving them even more bereft of resources for anything new.

In this book I will suggest that many of our traditional ways of doing things need some Second-Curve thinking – capitalism itself, the economy and how we measure it, education, work and how it is organised, marriages and families, democracy and government. It is not my purpose, nor is it in my competence, to prescribe in detail what the next curve should be in any of these areas. That can only be done by those who are currently riding the first curve or who might start the second. My purpose is only to challenge and question and, occasionally, to suggest or provoke. I want the world that my grandchildren will live in to be a different and a better place. If my suggestions seem outrageous, ill-considered or dangerous then so much the better. If the ideas in this book provoke arguments among colleagues and friends and if the book acts as a trigger to some to start thinking about the Second Curve then I will be well satisfied. 'How do I know what I think until I hear what I say?' the Irishman said.

For starters, consider the following:

The financial crisis of 2007–10 did more than disrupt economies around the world; it forced many to rethink their priorities in life, how they lived and why they lived. Organisations, particularly those in business, should start to re-examine their assumptions, questioning whether in an uncertain world it still makes sense to make the size of their enterprise so important. Can some businesses become too big to fail because of the damage to others that might result? Might it be wiser to aim to grow better without growing bigger? If economies of scale are crucial, is it necessary to own everything? Could the economies be achieved by non-competitive alliances instead? If so, how will these be managed and monitored?

Has money become too powerful? If Facebook can rustle up $19 billion from its own resources to buy up a possible competitor, if Google can use its wealth to corner all the artificial intelligence expertise around, are we seeing the need for a modern trust-busting Teddy Roosevelt? Is money in the new digital world a true reflection of value? Should money be allowed to influence voters in what are supposed to be democracies, but if not, how can political campaigns be financed? New problems for a new age where old solutions no longer work.

Modern youth may well sit looser to institutions, loath to sell their talents and their time in advance to soulless corporations. How then will the institutions engage with such people, given that they will still need their talents? How should society prepare these young people for self-sufficiency in such a world? Can schools, as institutions themselves, prepare people to live outside institutions? Will families remain the bedrock of society or will they, too, increasingly fragment into looser associations? Can emails and Skype, Facebook and Twitter compensate for physical connection? Can you indeed ever trust someone that you have never met, may never meet?

The questions rumble on. What will hold a society together? Will we dissolve into ghettos of religion and race or will we find something better than war or economic success to build a united country? Bigger than all these issues is that old philosophical conundrum – what are we striving for anyway, as individuals and as a society? Is selfishness necessary for economic growth, or could we find a better measure of success? Is altruism and a concern for others, what Adam Smith called sympathy, part of our nature or does it have to be learnt or acquired?

New thinking is not the prerogative of those in authority. They are often too wedded to their accustomed ways, to that first curve, to conceive that another way might be possible. The thinking could and should start with ourselves. I am sure that each one of us can make a difference – to our own lives, to the lives of those around us, especially our families, to the institutions to which we may belong, to the communities in which we live and even to the countries of which we are citizens. One of our faults is that we are too modest, too willing to believe that those in power know best.

I used to think that – until I taught some of them, then I knew that most of them were as ordinary as us. If we want to see a better society it has to start with us and in our own lives. The Second Curve is our chance to make up for any shortcomings on the first curve, to redeem ourselves and to show that we have learnt from the past in order to create a better future.

2

THE DIY SOCIETY

Does technology change the world?
Is it for better, or worse?

IN OR AROUND 1450 Johannes Gutenberg, a gold-
smith, discovered after years of experiment how to
make movable metal type to be used in a printing
press. A single press could now produce 3,600 pages a
day compared with just a few by hand copying. Within
a few decades people all over Europe were able to read
the Scriptures and other works in their own language
in their own homes. That simple fact changed the
structure of society. No longer did people have to accept
the words of those who could read, the priests and
those in authority. Now they could make up their own
minds. Gutenberg was not trying to change society,
only to add a Second Curve to his business, but as the
consequences rippled down through the generations
people everywhere began to appreciate the new freedom
of thought that this new technology gave them.

As John Naughton says in his book *From Gutenberg
to Zuckerberg*, who would have thought back then that

Gutenberg's invention would not only undermine the authority of the Catholic Church but also trigger a Protestant Reformation, enable the rise of modern science, create entirely new social classes and professions, even change our conception of childhood as a protected period in a person's life? It seemed unlikely that a new invention in Mainz would ultimately cause so much change, but there were many who felt that the foundations of their life had been washed away. Change is seldom welcomed by those in power.

Five hundred years later it has happened again. The internet started life as a device to enable the US Department of Defense to improve their internal communications, a local Second Curve. The World Wide Web was first used in a sceptical CERN in Switzerland to organise the internal telephone directory although its founder, Tim Berners-Lee, the modern Gutenberg, always had far grander ambitions for it, even when his colleagues told him that with a name like that it would never catch on. For Berners-Lee it was a way to connect the world, to give everyone everywhere a freedom to share and to choose. It was essential to his vision that it should be free, his gift to a disbelieving world. It is astonishing, now, to realise that it is only 25 years since its launch. Technology spreads faster today than in the 15th century. The dilemmas and challenges, however, are still the same.

As with Gutenberg's invention the computer, followed by the internet and all its offshoots, has given us freedom, but freedom with consequences. One of those consequences is the dislocation of the middle orders in the structures of commerce and society as individuals use their new freedom to bypass them, leaving organisations stranded, rather like towns bypassed by a new road. In 1992 I was invited to address the annual gathering of the British Booksellers Association. At that time they were worried about the proposed entry of Borders, the American chain of bookstores, into the British market. I told them that their real enemy was not another bookshop but a website, a concept that was then unknown to anyone outside the computer world. The idea that a website, not a bookstore, would be their competitor seemed to that conference to be a bit of science fiction. History was soon to make it all too real. That website, initially Amazon but soon followed by many others, allowed individuals to bypass the traditional channels of commerce, leaving traditional booksellers struggling to survive. The middle layer was disappearing and with it many jobs and a way of life. The bookselling example also suggested that the next changes in many industries would not come from within the industry but from somewhere completely different, from out of the blue. That's scary if you are in an industry planning its future.

Meanwhile the computer was taking many routine tasks away from their human agents, including the checking roles that used to be the job of many middle managers, taking the guts out of many organisations. The increasing sophistication of computers with so much more processing power enables them to analyse so-called 'big data' more speedily and accurately than humans. Computers can now detect intruders on a security system, identify fraud or diagnose disease more efficiently than any human expert. Much of the drudgery of a legal office can be done by computer. A lot of the work of the public sector is routine and begging to be computerised. Researchers in Oxford University suggest that 47 per cent of today's jobs will be replaced by computers within the next two decades – 250 million in just the next one, says the McKinsey Global Institute. By the time you read this these numbers may well look dated.

What will replace those 250 million jobs? Kodak at its height employed 145,000 people. Facebook employs just 6,000 while Instagram, when it was bought by Facebook for around $1 billion, employed just 13. Two years later Facebook paid $19 billion for WhatsApp with 55 employees but with half a million customers and growing. In earlier technology shifts the jobs that were displaced were quickly replaced by new ones. The women from the cotton mills could retrain as typists as work moved from factories to offices. This time the new jobs are not only very different, most of them do not yet exist. What then will we all do?

That's the bad news and it does not sound much like freedom. The good news is the power that individuals now have, with which they can use those bypasses to manage their own lives. It is becoming a do-it-yourself economy. We can not only buy books online, we can publish our own, should we wish to write any. We need no longer go anywhere near a physical bank; we can even start our own by creating a crowd-funding site. Kickstarter, one of the leading sites, began in 2009 and opened in Britain in 2012. You can, should you wish to take the risk, start your own currency. Bitcoin, Peercoin and Primecoin already exist as internet currencies with a defined amount whose value varies according to the demand, although the risk quickly overtook a couple of the early Britcoin exchanges. Or you can turn banker yourself via a peer-to-peer lending platform.

You don't have to leave home to go to university any more. With the help of the new free online courses offered by leading universities combined with imaginative video exercises you can, if you are diligent, shape your own degree. The Open University in Britain has long proved that distance learning can work well if it is disciplined. That said, you can also start your own academy in a subject of your choice, design the learning material, promote it and deliver it on the web. My wife has designed and taught her own photography course via the web to some lucky students. You can monitor your own health and diagnose your illnesses, using the Apple Watch if you want to know the time as well. You can download your favourite music almost free, but you can also make your own music available to others, also for almost nothing. Or you can turn hotelier by using Airbnb to rent out your spare rooms. The auction site eBay creates hundreds of thousands of virtual traders, buying and selling through the site.

Everything you can do as a customer you can also do as a supplier, even write your own computer game if you so wish. You can sell a seat in your car, a meal in your home, a parking space outside your house, a loan of your bicycle, even time with your dog, along with limitless other services in the newly christened 'sharing economy'. This new fashion is just one more example of the excluded middle, allowing you as an individual to bypass the conventional suppliers of these services by doing it yourself on the web. It is big business for some. By April 2014 Airbnb was valued by investors at $10 billion, bigger than Hyatt or the Intercontinental hotel groups, while the homeowners each earned an average of $7,530 in 2013 by renting out their rooms. Because the start-up costs are minimal, thanks to the internet, the number of new digital enterprises is legion, even though many of them are destined to fail. Time will tell, but it is doubtful whether many of these new businesses or services will create a lot of jobs even if they do succeed. Most of them will remain hobby businesses, pocket-money extras.

Sensing a change in the air, some of those suppliers who might be bypassed by the new passion for renting not owning are following suit. Home

Depot is renting out tools as well as selling them, Daimler is renting Smart cars by the minute, General Motors has invested in Relay Rides, a car-sharing firm. In London, escalating house prices are turning many into renters rather than owners. Is this the start of a new curve, one in which ownership is too expensive, too onerous, too hard to change? Is the rental economy part of the new Second Curve? Come to think of it, renting brings flexibility. Why tie yourself up in fixed assets of any sort when you can rent almost anything, use it and move on?

Whether we like it or not we are going to be forced to move into the DIY economy. Long years ago, working in the marketing department of Shell International, I found myself the very junior member of a group discussing the possible introduction of a new type of pump at our service stations, a pump which customers could work for themselves. Until then drivers had always had their tanks filled by attendants. 'It will never be accepted,' some said, 'no one will want to get their hands dirty.' 'We will have to offer a big discount,' said others. They were all wrong. People loved the new pumps. No more hanging around, waiting for attendants to finish the car in front, having to chat to them, even to tip them. We had successfully outsourced the job to the customer. Of course, supermarkets had got there long before. Others were soon to follow suit. Fedex makes you fill in your own documentation. Airlines want you to print out your own boarding pass, using your ink and paper not theirs. Ryanair fines you if you don't. We are exploited by our suppliers and we actually enjoy it because it gives us back control.

It not only puts us in control of our own affairs, it saves money. It pays to become your own lawyer, to file your own divorce papers, manage your own house sale, fight your own case in the small claims court. And we like it, most of the time. So we should expect the outsourcing to increase. Now, more and more, we are being asked to be our own doctor and nurse, to take responsibility for our own health. The Airedale General Hospital on the edge of the Yorkshire Dales serves 200,000 people over 700 square miles, many living in remote homesteads. Yet it manages to provide instant access to medical help 24/7 via telemedicine. Webcams and iPads, linked up to a secure network, have been installed in the homes of those with heart or breathing problems. Monitors allow them to monitor their own oxygen levels without leaving the house. The patients like it because they are in control and the savings are startling, a 69 per cent reduction in A & E visits and a 45 per cent fall in hospital admissions for people using the scheme.

Now that the technology exists to warn people when they are going into heart failure, to measure their heart rate and respiration, even how fast and far they walk or how obese they are, the responsibility falls back on the individuals to take the necessary remedial actions or to contact their doctor, probably through Skype or an app on their phone. The downside of all DIY is that being in control also means being responsible. When things go wrong it is most likely to be your fault. As I suggested in the Introduction, self-responsibility will be a feature of the emerging society. That will be uncomfortable for many who have grown up in a society that has assumed ever more responsibility for our personal safety and well-being, to the extent that we are tempted to assume that anything that goes wrong must be the fault of someone or something else. A DIY society reverses that. There will be no one to sue except yourself. Whether you consider that to be a good outcome or a bad one, it will undoubtedly be a shock for many as we move from what has gradually become a dependent society, an all-embracing welfare state, towards a more independent one. We will, for instance, have to assume more responsibility for our own financial planning. I gave no thought to pensions until it was almost too late. Luckily my first two employers had done so on my behalf. That will not happen to most of us any more unless we ask them to, nor will the state be able to pick up the pieces. As I will suggest in Essay 10, 'The Ponzi Society', we will have to take care of our financial future ourselves. For many that will be a very new curve.

When I was young and strapped for cash, DIY was what you did, because it saved money and your own labour cost nothing. I painted my own house, grew my own vegetables, mended our broken doors and fences. The finished work wasn't always high quality, even quite shame-making, but that was my responsibility and I had to live with it, telling myself that at least it had not cost much. Comfortingly, I told myself, we were more or less self-sufficient, albeit poor in financial terms. One of the consequences of that earlier industrial revolution was that many families had to move to the towns to be near the factories where the new work was. Removed from their plot of earth they could no longer be as self-sufficient as they had been. Their money now went less far, their poverty increased even though their wages went up.

The years passed for us. Older and a touch better off we hired others to do the work we used to do ourselves. For a time we lived out the old saying that it is the duty of the wealthy man to give employment to the artisan – and to blame him if it is not up to scratch. It did not feel as good, although the work was better done and the GDP of the country went up a notch. In fact that was how the developed world grew its economies, by taking activity out of the home and into the formal economy, getting others to do for money what used to be done by oneself for free, whether it be home repairs, childcare and care of the elderly, cooking and cleaning, car maintenance, financial accounting or entertainment.

Now, with the help of technology, many of those activities are being put back into the home again.

Hi-tech DIY is capital-intensive: those flat-screen televisions, sophisticated monitoring systems for the kids, robotic cleaners and so forth all cost money but they do make the chores less tedious. The result will be the reverse of the earlier movement. Employment will drop a bit, particularly in the domestic service sector. The capital goods sector may improve, although much of it will probably be imported. More people will shrink back into their homes rather than go out on the town. Our homes will increasingly become work hubs as we start to exploit all the opportunities of the new DIY and sharing economies. The worrying thought is that we will see less of other people except on the screens of our phones or computers, even if we work in some sort of organisation. It is this aspect of the DIY Second Curve that I will explore in the next essay, because we are all going to have to find our way up this curve, whether we like it or not. Fortunately those most affected by it, the up-and-coming generations, are enthusiasts for it, so all should be well for the future.

3

THE NEW DISRUPTION

How will the information revolution change your life?

MY WIFE'S FIRST photographic book was a portrait of our country village, as it was a century ago and as it is now, the houses and the people. She titled it *Behind the View* because she wanted to show how, outwardly, nothing much had changed in 100 years, but behind the view much had changed. The view from our cottages over farmland is as it was then, but the owner of the land does not farm it, he contracts it out. The houses and cottages of the old village are still there with only a few additions, still called Poplar Tree Farm or Farm Cottages. The difference is the people who live in them and what they do. One hundred years ago everyone in the village of 700 people worked on the land or were connected to it. Our cottages were home to two farm labourers and their families. Today they house a writer and a photographer. Now there are only two farmers in the village and no farm labourers. People commute to work elsewhere or work from home. The village today is still home to

700 people, still looks the same but is very different behind the front doors.

Looking back, it was a great disruption. Nobody even 50 years ago could have imagined how much would change, or how. The positive message is that the village survived, even thrived. People adapted. They always do, in the end. In the process, however, the things they do to survive, pay their way and support their families will change, just as farmhands gave way to writers. Now we are in the middle of a new disruption. The landscape and the houses may continue to look the same but what the new forms of work will be we can only guess at.

In 2011 Thomas Frey, a futurist, tried his hand at it, listing the jobs of the future that don't exist today. They included waste data managers, responsible for de-cluttering our data stores, urban agriculturalists, avatar designers, privacy managers, nano-medics and organ agents, hired to find organ replacements around the world. In total Frey listed 55 potential new jobs that might arise over the next 30 years or so. Some of them, such as alternative currency bankers, are already around; others will follow even if they do not precisely match Frey's predictions. It is worth noticing, however, that most, if not all, of Frey's future jobs can be done by individuals on their own. They do not need large corporations to deliver their services, although they may work for them or alongside them.

It is not just the new jobs that we should be concerned with. The whole way that we will arrange our work and our lives is changing as a result of what Luciano Floridi, the intriguingly titled Professor of the Philosophy and Ethics of Information at Oxford University, calls the infosphere and others term the information revolution. This is the major new curve in society whose full implications are slowly dawning on us. We have no choice but to ride that new curve, confident, however, that we will adapt and survive as we always have, in the end. Back in rural Ireland 60 years ago information was very limited and communication difficult. Our phone number was Clane 6, a hint that there weren't many people to call, or to call us. There was no television and a patchy radio signal. Petrol was expensive, cars were scarce and many still drove pony traps or cycled. It seemed to me at the time that we were still living in the world that Jane Austen described, a small self-contained world, content unto itself. It was unexciting, to put it mildly.

Two generations later I can't complain of boredom. We find ourselves swimming in a sea of information with almost infinite possibilities to communicate with whomever we want, or, indeed, sometimes do not want. All recorded knowledge is there for the taking, even much that was intended to be safe from prying eyes. Everyone can potentially know everything, be in contact with everyone. Google and Wikipedia are the first ports of call on any new question. Twitter connects me with my most authoritative friends. I have no excuse for ignorance. Nor does anyone else. Everyone can know what I know, often what I think as well. All that is lacking is the time. The new future is both exciting and daunting. Daunting because when information is open to all it redistributes power, replacing hierarchies with networks, taking politics beyond politicians and turning employees into free agents. It is exciting because it opens up more connections, erodes boundaries, encourages exploration and initiative. Information used to be the source of power in organisations when it was rationed and curtained off, available only to the licensed ones, but when all information is potentially open, where there are no secrets, power and authority evaporate. That plays havoc with organisational structures. With relationships too, when no secrets are safe.

Perhaps it will ultimately be for the best. Open secrets can increase trust. I recall an experiment in one organisation where they asked everyone to estimate the salaries of their colleagues. In every case each thought the others were paid more than they actually were. So they decided to make all salaries public to remove any possible resentments. Openness frees up organisations just as it did in Gutenberg's day when the power of the priesthood was undone by the circulation of the Bible to all who wanted it. Then religion finally belonged to the people, not to the priests. The latter did not, however, give up without a fight, nor will the modern custodians of information. Religion tried to use the Inquisition to re-establish control. Edward Snowden and other hackers have demonstrated that there can be few real secrets any more but the establishment is fighting back, also probably in vain. Here too, when what was secret is revealed the result is often not as explosive as everyone expected. Transparency is not always as risky as it seems.

On the other hand, the freedom that the infosphere gives us can be confusing and challenging. When I read an email or a tweet, if I do not know the writer, I cannot know where he is, or even if it is he and not she or they. Anonymity is the shield of the scoundrel but also the weapon of the adventurous. We can now be who we like, address whom we wish, explore where we want. There are lurking dangers there if we experiment too freely or share our private worlds too widely. No wonder that Professor Floridi's job title includes the study of the ethics of information because, in the free-for-all world that we are entering, right and wrong need redefining. Self-responsibility becomes more important when authority has lost its power. When there is no one to tell you what to do, the why and how of our lives is more than ever up for grabs, something that I will explore in the final essay of this book.

Like all of these social revolutions it is easier to discern them and their effects when looking back at them than when living through them. The Industrial Revolution of the 19th century was not given that name until long after it was all in place. What is certain is that the social disruption that followed the new technologies then will almost certainly be replicated now. The old power structures get demoted. New ones emerge, but take time to assume their responsibilities. Productivity falls for a time as we adapt to new technology and the new areas and types of work, a phenomenon known as the Solow effect after the economist Robert Solow, who first noticed this phenomenon. All these signs are already appearing in most developed societies. Work is being redistributed to smaller units which are less productive at first. It will take time for them to adjust and to grow. What seems certain is that old solutions are unlikely to work any more. Most of the old structures of organisations will soon have outlived their usefulness.

Social disruptions, as Frey's list of new jobs demonstrates, bring new opportunities as well as problems. What is also true, however, is that, as in that earlier revolution, these new opportunities are not likely to tempt those who are currently employed in the disappearing middles of the old order. The new jobs will go to new people, to the young who will, hopefully, grow up with the new skills that are needed. Meanwhile the bulk of the old jobs that will be left for the current workforce will be in areas where technology can help but not take over. These are the jobs where creativity is key or where personal attention is needed, in nursing, health care, social work and care of the elderly, but also in the performing arts, tourism and entertainment as an increasing number of older people move into the leisure stage of life. It is estimated that there will be an extra 2.7 million new jobs needed in social care in Britain by 2020. One piece of encouraging news is that there are now 72,000 apprenticeships on offer in that sector, most of them already taken up. The challenge here is how to make the best use of the new technologies. In many cases that will involve creating a Second Curve for each profession, with all the difficulties and resistance that will cause.

There will also still be jobs in architecture and management, in advertising and marketing, teaching or mentoring, counselling and arbitration, and in businesses such as yoga or meditation, craft work and design. There will still be shops, estate agents and travel agents and other outlets in our shopping malls as the web sellers realise that a physical outlet is often needed to complement their websites. People like to try on the dress before buying it, see the dishwasher as it really is, meet the travel agent in person, even if the final sale is done on the web. Cars will still be manufactured, oil wells drilled, crops grown and harvested, pills composed and packaged, but in every case the information component will be the bit that makes the difference. Here, too, relationship and management skills as well as technical ones are going to be needed, with computers and robots doing much of the routine and heavy lifting work. It will be work for brains and fingers not muscles.

Most worrying, to some, is the possibility that the infosphere is going to make many choices and decisions for us, without our say or even our knowledge, that the computer will be our master rather than our slave. Quantum computing, when it gets going, will take many tasks out of human hands, massaging big data bundles at vast speeds to tell us the quickest, shortest or cheapest ways to analyse what is going on in our bodies, to manage traffic and distribution systems in real time or help cars drive themselves. Increasingly there will be bits of our lives that will be managed invisibly by algorithms, mathematical formulae that you do not know are there. Unseen computers are already detecting trends and tastes in our lives that we were unaware of, knowing more about us than we know ourselves, deciding our food baskets, our new wardrobes and even our preferred partners. We will always be able to override their selections but it is all too easy to go along with Amazon's recommended choice when you are in a hurry. As much as anything, inertia will be the computer's friend.

It then gets more sinister. Fibre-optic cables underground can be used to detect the slightest motion within ten feet of them. Unknown to us our movements can be tracked both by cameras and by those unseen cables. Our mobile phones are really high-powered computers in our pockets, recording everything we say or write, to whom we send it and where from. Laws can try to protect our privacy but they can also license the invasion without our knowledge. Does this mean that the new freedoms given to us by the new technologies have been balanced by the loss of control of much of our life? Can there be secrets any more? Has the algorithmic society arrived?

Some of the freedoms we consciously give away, happy to live in a world of direct debits where our money is sucked out of our accounts without us noticing, unless we are vigilant. Having failed to change my passwords, my email account was hacked and all my contacts stolen. My bank received instructions to send some thousands of pounds to addresses I had never heard of. Carelessly handing my credit card to a waiter to take away to pay the bill, I later found that I had apparently bought an expensive flat-screen television the next day. None of these experiences is now uncommon. Identity theft was a term unknown to my parents, but then so were computers. Delighted by the new 'internet of things', we snap up the app that will park your car for you or find your lost key; the internet-enabled home even has a device that allows your phone to unlock your door without your having to take it out of your pocket. It is gadget heaven, until someone else gets hold of that phone. Every Second Curve brings its own learning curve, until we eventually work out how to live with its consequences.

The spread of social media has enriched many rela-tionships. When our teenage children went wandering the world 30 years ago we lost contact for weeks. Just as well, perhaps, when we heard of their scary adventures on their return. Now they can be in constant touch even in the midst of faraway jungles. But there are downsides and dark sides to it all. Social media creates what some have called a dissatisfied narcissism as we endlessly seek an elusive perfection, like wearing all your clothes at once. The social media knows no deference and carries with it no real sense of responsibility, no awareness of its impact on others. What is happening right now becomes dominant, skewing our priorities, neglecting the longer-term impact. A world of instantaneous messaging and simultaneous multi-viewing, of data on demand but without analysis, can, if we are not careful, lead to a shallow and self-centred take on the world, a Twittering world where no one has the concentration or time to take in more than a paragraph. Living in the present is all very well, but if we fail the Marshmallow Test we will short-change our future.

Walter Mischel, a leading expert on self-control, devised the Marshmallow Test almost 50 years ago. In an empty room he presented young children with a choice: take one marshmallow now or wait a while and have two. It was a test of deferred gratification. After observing the later lives of the children he was convinced that deferred gratification was crucial to a successful life, to better social functioning and to a greater sense of self-worth. If he is right then the world of instant constant communication is endangering the successful futures of our young. I discuss some further implications in Essay 15, 'The Necessity of Others'. We, and they, need to be careful.

We need to be careful too of the darker side of the infosphere. It facilitates conspiracy and assembly, lawful or not. Cyberbullying, sexting and trolling were all new words a few years ago, new words signalling new dangers. One suspects that any attempts to control the perpetrators will be in vain. They will always be one step ahead. It will, as always, be up to us to take care. More insidious, because less noticed, is the gradual takeover of internet traffic by the large corporations. Whereas initially there were thousands of companies generating content for transmission, it now seems that 30 companies control over half of all internet traffic in the USA, getting fewer all the time. Once again the elephants have trampled on the fleas. That does not stop us using the web for our own purposes, of course, but we may increasingly find ourselves seduced by the stream of 'infotainment' coming our way from those 30 corporations. Instead of being a force for innovation, as we hoped, we may increasingly lie back and enjoy Netflix, YouTube, Google, Facebook and Twitter and all that they and their successors will offer us. The internet will have changed us into couch potatoes instead of entrepreneurs. That is the Second Curve that we do not want to ride.

Sometimes, like many of my vintage, I yearn for the simpler Jane Austen world in which I grew up, forgetting how slow and inconvenient much of it was. I wrote my first book in longhand, laboriously crossing bits out and inserting others in the margin, handing the resulting scribbles to my wife to type out on a portable typewriter, since nobody had suggested that anyone with my level of education would ever need to type anything themselves. It was a better book. I took more care because there was no cut-and-paste, no easy way to correct mistakes. Maybe a backlash is coming. Motorola has produced a new minimalist phone that makes calls and messages and not much else. Organisations are instituting email-free days. Soon, maybe, we will have cool spots as well as hot spots, places where nothing electronic will work. Instead of messaging each other across the table we might start to talk to each other again. Meditation is fashionable. My day starts with half an hour of walking meditation, in the open air. It clears the head before I get immersed in busy-ness.

The infosphere is a Second Curve that we didn't create and didn't plan, but one whose consequences we cannot avoid. Second Curves don't just change products and processes, they change relationships, organisations and politics. What seems sure is that the world that our grandchildren will work in will have very different organisations and very different life options than the ones I knew. Whether they will be better or nicer is another question.

4

THE WORKPLACE

What? Where? Who? and How?

WE HAVE TO contemplate a day when most factories
– if they are still called that – are largely staffed by
robots and call centres by talking computers, when
cars, lorries and trains are increasingly driverless, when
cooking is fully automated, the menu of your choice
brought by robot to your table, when most shopping
is online and entertainment on tap in your lounge or
bedroom. Much of our lives will be organised by algorithms and computer-controlled systems. It will be,
some say, a world where humans service the machines
rather than the other way round, science fiction become
fact. The new servants, better termed technicians, will
need to be highly skilled, but, and here's the rub, few
in number.

I am unconvinced. Computers and the internet of
things may remove some of the drudgery of life, but
we humans will not lightly surrender our lives to
machines, particularly when those machines may one
day be able to think for themselves. People will always

congregate to create things, to gain power or influence, to make money or to help and care for others, things machines cannot do. There will always be organisations and places of work with the conflicts and excitements that come when people seek to do things together. The world of work may look different and be arranged and organised differently but there will always be organisations of some sort. Organisations, however, are just ways of connecting people and now that there are so many other ways to connect beyond face-to-face encounters we will see the physical aspect of the organisation changing rapidly. It has always struck me as odd to watch all those streams of people pouring out of railway stations in order to sit in their box-like cubicles communicating with similar folk in other boxes by email, telephone or messaging when they could do it equally well from home, or from a local work hub.

Why do they do it? Offices are expensive and most are unoccupied not only at night but for much of the day while their occupants are out and about with clients or suppliers or sitting in meetings. To save on space offices are becoming like London clubs, good for meeting and eating and with spaces allocated to activities but only to a few essential individuals to use as their own. To draw their people into them, these new corporate clubhouses are designed to be stylish, even luxurious, with the latest communication and display devices, along with restaurant-style food. The thinking is that people do need to rub up against each other in

physical space from time to time to encourage serendipity and a shared culture. If casual meetings can no
longer be around the copying machine or the water
cooler, because those disappeared along with the offices,
then let them happen in the club rooms. Serendipity
is important, as is a sense of cohesion, but, as one
executive said to me, not every day. Why not confine
it to the three midweek days?

Some fight against the trend, partly because they
believe that you can't have too much serendipity and
partly because the hot-desking involved in the club
concept is not popular with those who still see the
office as a home from home. They want to build their
own individual space with their familiar household
gods and photos. These organisations go the other way,
making the workplace into an all-purpose campus-type
centre for work and recreation à la Google. Not only
is this hugely expensive, it may be that not all people,
or perhaps even most, want to lose themselves so
completely in their workplace.

The new variety of the physical workplace, from
office to club to hub to home, is one sign of a changing
workforce. The day of the mass employment organisation, with everyone under one uniform corporate
umbrella if not one physical roof, could be the first to
go. That may be no bad thing. Size breeds inhumanity,
reducing individuals to mere human resources, costs in
the account books. In the lower regions of these vast
armies one can feel like a very small cog in a huge

machine. At their worst they can be prisons for the human soul. The likes of Walmart and G4S have a huge headcount but are actually collections of small organisations, not the conglomerations of old, massed behind the factory gates. Other large organisations, my old oil company included, are gradually going federal although they don't necessarily call it that, aiming to be big where it matters and small where they can in order to keep it human and flexible. They look for a requisite variety of shape and size and style, while keeping it all connected by company websites, emails, Skype, messaging and even the old-fashioned telephone turned smartphone.

The new fashion for this virtual connectivity means that our laptops are effectively our offices and, of course, they need not reveal to anyone where we physically are. Convenient though that is, it also means that I can never leave my office. Unless I am disciplined enough to turn off all the technological gadgets I am more enslaved, not less. It is not religion that is today the opium of the people, as Karl Marx once suggested, but the smartphone. Where once people took comfort in their rosary or worry beads now some seem unable to sit without gazing at the small screen in their hand, twittering to all and sundry, pressing 'reply all' too automatically and 'delete' too seldom. The new worry is that people are over-communicating because of this new peripatetic office, leaving too little space for reflection and contemplation.

Looking ahead to the next curve it already seems clear that work is going to be organised in a range of different ways. There will always be the elephants, the large organisations that will still account for the largest part of any national output. As I suggest in Essay 8, 'The Citizen Organisation', they and their constituent bits will be shamrock-shaped, with most subsidiary functions separated out either to independent contractors or to subsidiary businesses owned but not managed by the centre. There will also be numbers of what I once called fleas, or the third leaf of the shamrock. These are specialist individuals or small partnerships who sell their skills and expertise to organisations but are not directly employed by them. They are often specialists of one sort or another, but can also be main contributors to the operation while maintaining their independence. The big organisations are discombobulating into bundles of semi-independent groupings.

I am a flea riding on the back of an elephant. As an author I am a small part of the intellectual property at the heart of my big and global publishing house. They need me and others like me as much as I need them, but they would not want to employ me any more than I would want to be employed by them. Instead I am paid by results, with a little up front if I am lucky. It suits us both, although to outsiders it might seem odd that a business should be happy not to own the major part of their intellectual assets. Since this core part of their operation is already outside the organisation there is, in theory, no reason why everything else might not also be contracted out, leaving a few coordinators, perhaps the commissioning editors, in the middle. Welcome to the pure contractual organisation, the box of contracts masquerading as a community, the shamrock with a closely trimmed central leaf.

I have often wondered why more individuals with valuable specialist skills do not do as I do and step outside the organisation, selling their skills or intellectual property back into the organisation instead of giving it away for a salary. I can foresee groups of specialists, even whole research centres, or coteries of medical specialists, forming independent groups and contracting their work back to the organisation, trading security for independence, better rewards and more control. The attractions of the contractual organisation are clear, to both parties. For the organisation, overheads are lower. There is more flexibility. If one of the separated bits is not working as well as it should the contract need not be renewed. But it is also risky. The bits can leave to go elsewhere. The bar to entry for new competitors has now been lowered, any newcomer can hire the same outsiders. New publishers can spring up overnight, even working initially from their kitchen at home. Critically, however, there is no sense of community in a contractual organisation, no core values, nothing to inspire loyalty. Where contracts are key the spirit is lost.

Nevertheless it may only be a matter of time before the contractual organisation becomes the norm. It will be a sad day. The work organisation has been the main community for many, even if it wasn't always, or even often, as people-friendly as it should have been. Already those whose personal assets are highly valued, people such as bankers, film actors and sports stars, make a share of the profits a condition of their employment. This form of performance-related pay, where the contribution of a single member or a group can be identified, seems bound to grow along with the bargaining power of key talent. In the growing world of talent businesses employees will be increasingly unwilling to sell the fruits of their intellectual assets for an annual salary, even a big one. They will become independent fleas, or groups of fleas.

For the fleas, even the glamorous ones, the risks are clear. What they offer may be excellent; the challenge is to find enough people who want it and are prepared to pay for it. If the new fleas can start by selling their skills back into their old organisation they are fortunate, but even then they will soon need to find more customers. Marketing becomes as important as delivery. Those working in the service sector, as most fleas do, need customers much more than they need investment. A second-hand van, a computer and some basic equipment is enough for many to get started, all bought with the credit card. There are other problems, however. Many will have worked in businesses but been shielded from the harsh realities of business, the crucial importance of cash flow, the difficulty of setting the right price, the control of creditors, all things they may never have been involved with in their days of employment. There is also the delusion of grandeur that many new fleas suffer from, hiring office space and secretaries before they find their first customers, designing impressive websites and promotional literature when reality suggests that early customers have to be found through recommendation and word of mouth. Success often comes more slowly than planned but, in the end, most find that the freedom more than compensates for the insecurity. Our son is an actor, the worst of all flea occupations because you have so little control of your future, even when well established. Work is sporadic for most and unpredictable. He does it only because it is what he loves to do. More and more I think that we will all live the equivalent of actors' lives at some point in our life's journey.

Fleas can often combine their skills with others to form what looks like an organisation but is in fact just a bundle of flea contracts. Our own local builder suggested that we paid his suppliers and all the individual craftspeople separately if they were below the VAT level. That way we saved money and he saved on administration. A rule of thumb for small start-ups seems to be: don't employ them, hire them in as and when needed. Interestingly, according to an *Ideal Home* census, whereas in Victorian times one in seven households employed domestic help, it is now one in four, but almost all as self-employed individuals: the gardener, driver, caterer and cleaner.

One of the unanticipated but, in hindsight, inevitable consequences of the increasing array of taxes and regulations on employment is a growth in self-employment. The number of fleas is growing fast, up to 15 per cent of the total workforce in Britain, and that is only the ones we know about. Eighty-three per cent of the increase in employment in Britain since 2007 has been in fleadom, or *self*-employment; many of the new fleas are women, some of them unwilling, forced out of organisations, but most of them choosing the freedom to pursue their own path, made easier now that so much work is information-based in one way or another. Since much of their work will be for cash it is possible that the country is richer than we think: 6 per cent richer is the estimate of some economists.

Many of the fleas are over 60 with the mortgage paid off, the children gone, when overheads are lower and the risks reduced. Freed from the organisation by choice or by compulsion they are still active, still eager to contribute in some way or other. Retirement is not everyone's utopia, not yet anyway. Work, as we now know, keeps one healthy, active and, above all, involved and interesting. It is the best antidote to ageing and its accompanying ills, and it matters not whether the work involved makes money or is done for charity, is for the community, for personal pleasure or, in many cases, the care of a loved one. For many, however, some form of self-employment is becoming an essential top-up to an inadequate pension. It is a situation that will become increasingly common as the population ages. Put together a work portfolio, I tell such people, a collection of different types of work, or a variety of clients, then if one client or one project fails or ends it isn't final, there are all the others. These days I meet many a portfolio person with a clutch of different business cards to reflect their various roles. It makes for a more interesting life than that one job they used to have.

Second Curves have a way of creeping up on one. Already 93 per cent of all the businesses in Britain are microbusinesses, employing less than five people, often just one person or a couple. In total they only produce 3 per cent of the national GDP but in aggregate they employ more people than the whole of the public sector. Socially, and therefore politically, they matter, yet most of the structures and systems of society are built on the assumption that almost everyone works in an organisation of some sort. It is through organisations that the bulk of our taxes are collected, health and safety measures applied, sick leave and holidays paid for, jobs protected and pensions financed. Governments would like to push everyone back into the organisations, but the organisations don't want them and most of the fleas have no desire to go there.

Changing the metaphor, I have called this new growth in self-employment and microbusinesses the acorn economy. Most of the acorns will remain just that, acorns, some will get trampled underfoot, but a few may grow into tall oak trees employing or engaging many other workers. Sadly, that is often the only time that governments start to notice them. Governments need to remember that without acorns there would be no oak trees.

Whatever governments may wish, the reality is that in Britain today less than half of all adults of working age are in full-time employment. The others are self-employed, employed part-time, unemployed, in education or 'economically inactive': busy at home working often as unpaid carers of children or parents. The acorns and the self-employed fleas are of all kinds, some of them unconventional. The British government has begun to follow other European countries in adding the estimated earnings of drug dealers and prostitutes to their gross national income. After all, every little helps, and these earnings turned out to be not so little. In 2009 it was estimated that there were 60,879 working prostitutes in Britain, a strangely precise estimate, earning, in total, £5.3 billion. Drug dealers made £4.4 billion. Illegal fleadom is profitable, particularly if the fleas don't pay their taxes. More conventionally, when interviewed recently by a television crew I discovered that they were all – including the presenter and producer – self-employed, and pleased to be so. The strange truth is that if you have a so-called 'proper' full-time job today you are in a minority. The world has changed and few have noticed.

I was talking to an advertising executive in my home. He had been made redundant at age 48 and was indignant at the ageism of society. 'There aren't any jobs now for people like me, at the peak of my life,' he said, 'it's outrageous.' Just then the electrician who was working on a fault in the house put his head around the door – 'I have to be off now,' he said, 'got to go to another job.' 'There you are,' I said to the advertising executive, 'that's what a job means for many these days – a customer or a project, not a niche in an organisation. Find yourself some customers and you will have lots of those electrician-type jobs.' Sixty per cent of Britain's registered businesses, I pointed out, have no employees, just the proprietor. He was not comforted.

My parents were always home for lunch when I was growing up. I thought that was normal because so were most of the people we knew. My father was the Protestant rector of a small Irish parish. The others were farmers, doctors, a couple of horse breeders, an artist and the local shopkeeper who closed the shop for a couple of hours in the middle of the day. It was a long time before I realised that most people were away from home all day in another kind of home, an office or factory of some sort. When I found myself going out to work I envied my father his study, his very private place, and resolved to have my own one day, but for the next 30 years an office was my not-so-private study, almost a second home, where I spent more of my waking hours than in my true home. No wonder my children thought me a stranger.

Life comes round in circles. Today I have my study and my wife has hers. We both go to them every morning, emerging for coffee, lunch, tea and supper. More and more of us are now working *from* home if not always *at* home, even when we are employed. A neighbour works for a small electrical engineering business. The dozen or so engineers work from home, coordinated from a tiny office many miles away where they seldom go. According to Reuters some 10 per cent of people work from home every day and another 10 per cent do so one or more days a week. These numbers apply only to people in registered businesses. They do not include voluntary workers, hobby workers, home care workers, all the so-called non-economic activities. Then there are those who have no office because they work full-time at their clients' location or en route to it: electricians, plumbers, teachers, taxi drivers, lorry drivers, nurses, pilots, actors and many more. They may not have a room to call their own but they often share a common space to take breaks and socialise. Like so much else in the world ahead the workplace is increasingly going to be what we make it. Work is what we do, not where we go. The Second Curve has already started. Where it will lead us is the new uncertainty.

5

THE MARKET

Is it proving to be a false god? Where can we trust it?

MARKETS ARE USEFUL places. They are the easiest
and best ways to balance supply and demand. Without
them we would have to leave it to bureaucrats to do
the balancing task. As the Soviet Union eventually
realised, bureaucrats don't do it all that well. Markets
also encourage competition and that in turn promotes
innovation. In fact it is hard to see how society could
work or progress without its markets. But there are
downsides. Markets do not always work as well as they
should, as I shall demonstrate. People exploit them if
they can. Nor do they work in all situations. Some
things are not for sale, or should not be, like love or
brides for example. Other things are literally priceless,
like the air we breathe, which does not stop some
trying to charge for them.

More crucially, a market ideology distorts our priorities, even corrupts us, some would say. By a market
ideology I mean the belief that the best way to run
anything is to create a market. That means putting a

price on the end products and provoking competition. The result has to be that money becomes the measure of all things and turns everything, including parts of ourselves, into commodities for sale. Some are happy to sell their bodies, or their body parts; some have to do so in order to live. Others sell their connections to those who could use them. I know authors who charge a fee to endorse another author's book. How valid would that endorsement be? It is the dilemma of princes. If you are rich enough or important enough to buy the time or the approval of anyone you want, how will you know how genuine their feelings really are? Once you start to calculate the costs and benefits of everything you do you will be no better than a robot. Indeed a robot might well make better calculations than you.

If everything is for sale it accentuates the difference between rich and poor. Recently my wife and I were in Malawi, documenting a microfinance initiative, visiting the villages where the women who had been given those microloans to start a business lived. Their homes were simple mud huts, so small that they needed all the floor space for their large families to sleep on at night. They had no possessions. Nobody had. All were equal, different only in their personalities. Our sole concern was that some of the entrepreneurial women might upset this harmonious state by becoming too successful, because money creates differences. Sad but true. Markets are useful, but not for everything. Nor do they always work as they should.

My scepticism was aroused on the day of my first lesson in economics. 'Let us assume a perfect market. . .' the lecturer began. The assumptions, it became clear, included comprehensive and perfect information, available to all, purely rational competitors who thought only in economic terms and who were concerned only with finding an agreed price, with no interest in longer-term consequences or other aspects of the deal and, not least, a neutral means of negotiation. Dream on, I thought at the time, the world is not that simple.

It was all at odds with my first experiences of the market when I started work in the sales department of an oil company in Malaya, as the country was then called, 60 years ago. 'Your first assignment,' said the sales manager, 'is to fix the sale prices of our lubricants range for the next year.' I knew nothing about lubricants or the country so, rather dumbfounded, I said, 'I don't think, sir, that I am quite qualified to do that yet.' 'Nonsense,' he replied. 'All you have to do is get out the list of lubricants, take it down to accounts, ask them for the direct costs of each, add on a sum for our overheads, which they will give you, put our profit margin of 15 per cent on top of that and add it all up. Simple stuff, but it will introduce you to one part of our business.' 'But. . . That's almost immoral,' I stammered. 'Why so?' he asked. 'Well,' I replied, 'it means that the more we spend the more profit we make. That can't be right.' 'No, that's business,' he said, 'if you can get away with it. You'll soon learn.'

We got away with it because our only competitor had a much smaller share of the market and therefore higher unit costs, so was happy to go along with our rather extravagant habits. If they had initiated any sort of price war it would have been prohibitively expensive for them as well as us. What sort of market is that? In later years I observed more of this follow-the-leader pattern in business. It is not that similar businesses actively collaborate, rather that they calculate that it is too costly to rock the boat. I used to wonder why, in big cities, many of the trades used to cluster together, all the diamond merchants in Hatton Garden in London, all the gold dealers in one street in Dubai, all selling much the same products at the same price. Perhaps, I surmised, they wanted to ensure that no one broke ranks, that their hold on the market was not challenged, that price wars did not happen, because they damage all the players. You could argue, and I often do, that something similar happens in the financial sector, where no one challenges the huge fees that the investment banks charge or dares to call the bluff of those who claim that their bonuses have to keep pace with their competitors. It is in everyone's interest, except that of the customer, that everyone keeps rank and follows the leaders.

Later, when I was studying in America, my wife decided to join up with a friend back in London to sell brass rubbings, copied from the tombs of English knights and squires of old, to the housewives of Boston.

The friend in England would do the rubbings and then print them by the silk-screen process onto strong parchment-like paper. She would despatch these to Boston where my wife would turn them into wall hangings (they were typically four feet long) and sell them through the local clubs and societies. The question was – what price? I calculated that their finished cost, excluding my wife's labour which was free, would be $3 maximum. Add on a decent mark-up of $1 or 33 per cent and you got a sale price of $4 each.

My wife, who has always been better at business than me, thought that this was far too little, so she gave the problem to the marketing course where I was studying. They did a rudimentary market survey and recommended $40 on the grounds that the scrolls would only sell if they were promoted as a luxury product. Horrified at such profiteering, I insisted that we keep it to $20, and even this seemed a bit over the top. She sold enough to give us very a nice holiday in California at the end of my studies but I believe we might well have more than doubled our money if we had followed the advice we were given.

I have since observed that price is often taken as an indication of quality. I have friends who automatically go for the most expensive alternative on the assumption that it is likely to be the best. I myself, caught up in a difficult law case, felt that our medium-priced law firm would have to be replaced by a more expensive one who would, we assumed, do a better job. In the end,

I don't think they did, but when you are uncertain it can seem the safest way to go, albeit the most expensive. For a time I wandered the world as a conference speaker. It seemed to me that if I were to undercut, by half, the outrageous fees that some speakers charged I would get more invitations. It did not happen. The clients marked me down as being obviously in the second league. I raised my fees and we prospered mightily for a time. But I always knew that it was wrong to take such advantage of an imperfect market.

Perhaps all markets are imperfect. Maybe the spot market for crude oil or the various commodity and metal exchanges work better, where information is clear and the trading mechanism neutral. Well, maybe. But 50 years ago I acted as the secretary of a small group of very large men, a Belgian from the Congo, an American from Chile and an Englishman from Rhodesia. They would meet every six months in one of Paris's most luxurious restaurants to set the producer price for copper on the London Metal Exchange. The producer price from the main producers set the floor price for the metal and so ensured the stability of the market. It was, I was assured, all perfectly legal. My job was only to note down the price they agreed on, in case they forgot or chose to mis-remember. An odd sort of market, I thought at the time, but I could see that it made sense to fix a major piece of it.

There are other problems with markets. Markets that compare costs but not prices are illusory. Visiting

Hungary in the days when it was under communist rule, I remarked on the fact that they had two fertiliser plants for the whole country. 'Surely,' I said, 'it would be cheaper to have just one since there are obvious economies of scale in this industry.' 'But then we would have to work out what was the right cost level for fertiliser manufacture,' they replied. 'This way they set the standard for us by competing.' Point taken, I thought to myself, although it would be even better if they compared outcomes not just inputs, since it is the relation between the two that really matters. That was the flaw in their system. You can have a very cheap process producing a very bad product, as happened all too often in the Soviet regimes and still does in our own public sector. A proper market with measured outcomes as well as costs would signal that. That said, even those markets can lower standards, not raise them. More universities competing for students can tempt some to lower their admission standards and the criteria for their degrees. They can fill their courses but to the detriment of the eventual customers, the employers or the wider society. Nor is it obvious that the proliferation of TV channels and other media has improved the quality of the content, other than making more of it available to more people.

There are also areas in society where markets don't work at all, others where they work wrongly, and some where more of a market would help. You should not, for instance, create a quasi-market where none can exist naturally. The privatisation programme in Britain was an attempt to introduce some market principles into parts of the public sector. The end result was often the creation of local monopolies in areas such as water supply and rail, where only one operator per region is physically possible, or statewide monopolies such as the air-traffic control network. That then leaves it up to regulators to try to introduce some element of the price discipline that is the main advantage of a market. What, however, is to stop the organisation under review from behaving like the oil company I first worked in, claiming costs that they say are essential and adding their profit margin on top? It can be hard for a regulator acting alone to dispute them all. Ultimately the market discipline is intended to kick in when the fixed-term franchises are awarded but even those competitions are flawed. Some bids promise what in the end they can't deliver, others provide cost estimates that prove wildly optimistic, leaving the government, as provider of last resort, to pick up the pieces, making a farce of the whole exercise. Privatisation may deliver more efficiency but the cost of that efficiency can only be effectively challenged in a real market.

As it is, the sale of public utilities in Britain has usually resulted in bigger subsidies paid by government, higher prices to the consumers and, one assumes, comfortable profits for the suppliers, most of whom are foreign-owned. Few markets are perfect in the way that my economics teacher assumed. The problems continue. Markets don't work where the true outcomes are unpriced. What, for instance, is the true outcome of a prison? Or a hospital, or a school? In such cases the only thing priced is the cost, but, as I have argued, a cost without an outcome does not make a proper market. Cost comparisons will drive down costs but may not produce a better outcome. A hospital can free up beds by sending patients home before they are well enough, which would increase bed turnover but not the well-being of the suffering patients turfed out. Or it could cut its staff and so lower its costs but leave patients unattended.

Unfortunately the true outputs of prisons, hospitals and schools cannot easily be measured. Presumably the true test of a prison is the later life of the prisoners. How different has their life been over the next decade? If that could be measured it might encourage the prison management to invest more in retraining and rehabilitation than they do. A hospital might best be judged on the health of its surrounding population, or at least the continuing life of its patients. A school ideally needs to look at the progress of its students 20 years on. Since such measures of success are both difficult and impractical these organisations use substitute measures – the reoffending rate, the recovery time, the examination results, even though there is often no direct connection with the true longer-term purpose. The danger of such intermediate measures is that they can distort the real goals of the institution. Good grades do not necessarily lead to good citizens or good leaders. Teachers know that, but they are driven by the only things that can be measured, inadequate though it may be.

Intermediate measures fall foul of the MacNamara fallacy, as expressed by the US Secretary of Defense Robert MacNamara during the Vietnam War. It goes like this: The first step is to measure whatever can be easily measured. This is OK as far as it goes. The second step is to disregard that which can't be easily measured or to give it an arbitrary quantitative value. This is artificial and misleading. The third step is to presume that what can't be measured easily really isn't important. This is blindness. The fourth step is to say that what can't be easily measured really doesn't exist. This is suicide.

I would amend MacNamara's second step to read, 'to assume that what can be measured accurately leads to the desired outcome even if that cannot be measured'. That is the real missing link in the syllogism. Without that missing link it is a false market that leaves customers and policymakers in the dark, relying on hunches, not hard evidence. This is dangerous.

So, in the light of all this, was it not a touch naive of Alan Greenspan, the former Chairman of the US Federal Reserve, to say in his latest memoir, referring to the financial crisis of 2008, that 'I and other economic forecasters did not understand that markets are prone to wild and even deranging mood swings that are uncoupled from any underlying rational basis'? He, rather belatedly, confessed to losing faith in 'the presumption of neoclassical economics that people act in rational self-interest. To me it suddenly seemed that the whole idea of taking the maths as the basis of pricing that system [had] failed.'

No, Greenspan was not naive. Along with most of the business world and government, he believed that markets self-corrected. We could see it at work in the street markets. We were taught it at business school. It was that clever device by which selfishness became justified, even if the maxim of 'greed is good' was going a bit too far. Adam Smith, the godfather of economics, said it, so it had become a hallowed truth, almost the foundation stone of capitalism. So how could it all have gone so wrong?

Let us be clear from the start: Adam Smith did *not* say that the 'invisible hand' would allow self-interest to work for the good of all. He only mentioned that metaphor once in his book *The Wealth of Nations*, and that was to suggest that an invisible hand would incline a merchant to invest at home rather than in foreign lands.

His exact words are:

> By preferring the support of domestic to that of foreign industry, he intends only his own security; and by directing that industry in such a manner as its produce may be of the greatest value, he intends only his own gain, and he is in this, as in many other cases, led by an invisible hand to promote an end which was no part of his intention.

Just one example of how language can be twisted to mean what you want it to mean.

What Smith *did* say was that competition would return the price of anything to 'its normal price', which is, I suppose, much the same thing. But he also said that 'by acting according to the dictates of our moral faculties we necessarily pursue the most effectual means for promoting the happiness of mankind' and 'to feel much for others and little for ourselves; to restrain our selfishness and exercise our benevolent affections, constitute the perfection of human nature'. Bankers take note. Smith was a moral philosopher first and economist second. He was not giving licence to selfishness. Having also famously said that 'It is not from the benevolence of the butcher, the brewer, or the baker that we expect our dinner, but from their regard to their own interest', he later went on to suggest that it was actually in the interest of those businessmen to work to the self-interest of their customers. In short, enlightened self-interest works best for everyone. But he had no illusions: throughout history, he observed, we find the workings of 'the vile maxim of the masters of mankind: all for ourselves, and nothing for other people'. It could have been a trailer for Wall Street's 'Masters of the Universe' boast 300 years later. Markets, he insisted, needed good rules and strong government if they were to work in the interest of all.

I return, therefore, to my initial scepticism. Second-Curve thinking would accept that markets are useful, even essential, but that they need careful regulation and tight rules; that they do not work in all situations; that trusting to intermediate measures can be misleading; that an unquestioning belief in the power of the market to organise our lives is dangerous; and, crucially, that the value of much of life cannot and should not be expressed in financial terms. To do so is to turn us into commodities. We are all richer than that in ways that cannot be priced.

6

THE DILEMMAS OF GROWTH

Is more always better?

GROWTH IS ONE of those words with a halo around
it, suggesting that it is an undisputed good. But I
wonder. Can you have too much of a good thing? Is
more of everything good? Obviously not, when you
think of our diet. So what about the rest of life? Most
businesses would think it odd not to aim for growth,
but for ever? I was once, many years ago, in the world
headquarters of IBM. There was a chart on the wall
with two lines on it, projected into the future. One
line represented the estimated growth of the GDP of
the USA. The other was the projection of the worldwide
sales of IBM. At some distant point in the future, I
noted, the IBM line rose to cross the USA line. 'A nice
joke, surely?' I said to an IBMer. 'Not at all,' he replied.
'At our rate of growth it is quite possible.' Dream on,
I thought, how unreal can you get? Eternal growth has
to be a fantasy, unless there are forms of growth that
are not constrained by competition or lack of resources.
The rapid growth of data and of businesses built purely

out of information is one intriguing possibility, but it is hardly life-sustaining, even if profitable for some. Yet we have to ask, can life, work and society thrive without some economic growth?

Sometimes I hanker after a life in the Middle Ages when for most people nothing changed very much, when day succeeded day, changing only with the seasons, when everyone knew their neighbours and hardly anyone else, where your station in life was fixed at birth so you might as well make the best of it. Life was shorter, death more common and disease more frequent, but also simpler in that choices were limited. You made the most of what you had because there was little point for most people in seeking more or different. There is a comfort in simplicity.

The reality, of course, would have been very different. 'Solitary, poor, nasty, brutish and short', with 'continual fear', was Hobbes' description of life in what he called the state of nature, if mankind were left to its own devices. For a thousand years the economy hardly grew, but without growth there is bound to be constant competition for the available goods. Avarice does not disappear when there is not enough to go round. It gets worse. Growth allows choice, theoretically choice for all, progress for all, success of some sort for all. So in the end I settle for economic growth, despite all the competitive challenges for individuals and societies that come with it. A society without growth would become an envious and increasingly nasty society, with choices limited to a fortunate few. There are those who believe that the developed world has grown enough, that it is time for a pause to reflect and to let the rest catch up. The possibility of growth, however, is what keeps hope alive and despair at bay, no matter how well off we are.

But what sort of growth? Take economic growth to begin with. Economic growth has to be good since so much of our lives now rely on public goods and services to be paid by taxation. No growth with an expanding population means less for most, if not for all. But not all economic growth is beneficial. Growth that lavishes riches on a few but leaves the majority untouched is harmful. So is growth that leaves the world worse off for our successors by pillaging the environment and its resources. Growth that comes from improved productivity can result in unemployment as technology replaces people in the workplace. Having robots in place of people does not sound like progress for humanity. Unfortunately the common measure that we use for calculating economic growth does not take account of these qualifications.

GDP, the officially accepted measure of economic growth, is a dangerously flawed indicator in this respect. By brushing these concerns under the carpet, it allows those in authority to disregard them. GDP also ignores all activity where no money changes hands. As Robert Kennedy once said, GDP 'measures neither our wit nor our courage, neither our wisdom nor our learning, neither our compassion nor our devotion to our country: it measures everything in short except that which makes life worthwhile'. My vegetables, grown from my seeds, do not count in the calculation of the country's wealth, nor do those walks in the woods with the dog, so crucial to well-being, nor the hours spent by my children caring for their children. Such things could all be outsourced and paid for, thus boosting the GDP in a small way, but the activity would remain the same. Given that what is not counted does not count there must be a temptation for policymakers to pay too little heed to these uncounted matters. Then there are the payments in kind, the case of wine in exchange for some consultancy, the loan of a holiday cottage to compensate for some extra childcare, the safari we were given in place of a fee for a lecture in Africa. No space in my tax return for any of these things.

The flaws continue. Productivity reduces the prices of things, and with them the GDP, while often increasing their usefulness. Today's computers are cheaper but also better. On the other hand more highway accidents, more riots and more violence increase expenditure and therefore the GDP but damage society. Should such expenditure be subtracted from, not added to, the GDP, as the early proponents of GDP suggested? So much of what we get from the internet now is free or almost free and therefore is ignored by GDP. The informal or black economy is also uncounted. Undeterred, the Italians in 1987 decided to put it in, adding 20 per cent overnight to their GDP, overtaking Britain in the process. On the instructions of the EU Britain, along with the other countries, is now proposing to do likewise, officially adding 4 per cent to the gross national income by including the proceeds of illegal activities such as prostitution and drug-dealing. The suspicion must be that there is still a lot of undeclared income in the legal (grey) economy of small private enterprises. Given these and numerous other flaws in the measure it is a fool's errand to try to compare growth rates across different countries and currencies. In truth we do not know how well our economy or our society is really growing at any given time, even in economic terms, let alone human well-being.

A Second Curve badly needs a more satisfactory measure of a society's growth. In her illuminating book *GDP: A Brief but Affectionate History*, the economist Diane Coyle suggests that policymakers should adopt a dashboard of different measures. Sadly, politicians and the public yearn for the simplicity of a single number and, says Coyle, GDP is the best we have. Unfortunately it is used in public debate as the only measure in common use to assess our progress as a society. This is something it was never intended to do. We need Coyle's dashboard, complex though it will inevitably be. Perhaps in a Second Curve the public could be educated to understand that if you reduce complexity to simplicity you risk losing the message, tempting though the simplicity is. Governments should be encouraged to agree on a standard dashboard to measure the whole state of society. There are many measures on offer but none in public use. Australia has made a start with its annual publication *Measures of Australia's Progress*, where its citizens are consulted on what measures should be included. Where Australia leads more should follow.

Growth, however, is not just economic. I was once asked by a leading orchestra to help them with their plans for growth. I was puzzled. They seemed to me already to have a full complement of instrumentalists. Why would they want more violinists or trombone players? 'No, no,' they explained, 'we don't want to be any bigger, we want to be better, to expand our audiences, our repertory, our tours and, not least, as a consequence, our income.'

Better not bigger. I should have realised, because most of the organisations that I have found it most interesting to work with down the years have been ones where it made no sense to grow any bigger. The list includes schools, hospitals, sports teams, clubs, even families; once these had reached what seemed to be the optimum size any further addition would be pointless, might even be damaging. For these organisations the key question was not bigger but better, which, of course, begged the question, better in what way? We are back to those unanswered questions, why? what? and for whom?

Better not bigger is also the watchword of many of Germany's Mittelstand family businesses. These medium-sized businesses, mostly family-owned and mostly in manufacturing, are the mainstay of the German economy. They treat debt with suspicion, invest for the long term and shun the stock market. The market leaders in many niche products, their aim is to do one thing really well. They have, therefore, to invest in quality workmanship and research in order to survive. Typically located in small rural communities with a workforce in the hundreds rather than the thousands, they are human-scale businesses acutely aware of the importance of their workers, of their well-being and of their training. Jobs not profit are their priority, but profit follows, with much of it reinvested. As one family member said to me, 'You won't get rich in this family; it all goes back into the business.' If only there were more like them.

Conversely, publicly owned corporations, driven by their shareholders, tend to assume that bigger means better. 'Better for whom?' one has to ask. Too big can become boring, to the customer. When the same coffee shops, eateries, supermarkets and clothing shops feature in every shopping mall, it can begin to feel like the old Soviet Union where everyone wore the same clothes and ate the same food. We begin to ache for variety. Ultimately you can become too big for your own good, as McDonald's and Tesco were surprised to discover when their sales slumped disastrously in 2014. Nor is bigger necessarily richer. The research on business acquisitions consistently shows that most acquisitions do not add value to the shareholders of the purchasing company. They do, however, increase the overall turnover and the headcount. This boosts the power and prestige of those at the head of the organisation while at the same time diminishing the relative influence and significance of the individuals in the lower levels who now find themselves to be smaller cogs in a bigger machine. There are, of course, many good reasons for some mergers and acquisitions: to defend a market or to enter a new one; to find economies of scale or to rationalise production or distribution, where two can often do cheaper than one. But there often comes a point where bigger is too big, where the economies of scale bring less obvious psychological and social disadvantages, creating organisations that seem too big to be managed sensibly and effectively.

A case in point is G4S. Originally an amalgamation of two Danish and British security companies, it went on a buying spree in 2008, acquiring over a dozen companies, and has now ended up with more than 620,000 employees, making it the third largest private-sector employer in the world after Walmart and Foxconn in China. Both of the latter are closely focused on either retailing or manufacturing but G4S has spread its wings far wider, operating a range of security and associated services for governments and others in more than 125 different countries, effectively doing the jobs that governments don't want to do. In recent years it has been beset by scandals and failed deliveries, as when it fell down on the requirement to provide security personnel for the 2012 Olympic Games, leaving the British army to pick up the pieces. They were also accused of charging the Ministry of Justice for tagging offenders who were either dead, in prison, had their tags removed or had never been tagged, and agreed to pay £109 million to settle the affair. The suspicion must be that the centre cannot always know what its parts get up to. It must be hard, if not impossible, to create a common culture across such a diverse and huge swathe of businesses. Which prompts the question – why does it have to be so big when there are no obvious economies of scale or cross-fertilisation of skills? The suspicion must be that it is ego-driven from the top.

Growth by acquisition is tempting to those egos, but the result can be an oligopoly of a few big businesses dominating a sector of the economy and thwarting effective competition. When governments collude in the creation of these monster companies through their purchasing policies they are aiding and abetting the kind of oligopolies that they should be outlawing. One feature of the new information-based industries, such as Google or Facebook, which are financed mainly if not exclusively by advertising, is the user-takes-all phenomenon. Size is all-important so the leader effectively freezes out, or buys out, all would-be competing businesses. Anti-trust laws do not seem to apply where there are no competitors to collude with and regulators seem reluctant or unable to interfere.

In America the government once split up AT&T. Why not the new giants?

Big may be seductive but is it necessary or sensible? Back in the 1930s Ronald Coase argued the case for the large corporation. Keeping everything in-house, he suggested, lowered the transaction costs when compared with negotiating with separate outside businesses. Put simply, if you employed them you could tell them what to do. The result of applying the Coase argument was the integrated organisation, where everything connected with the output of the organisation was both owned and managed by it. Fifty years later he was awarded a Nobel Prize for his insight, just when new communication technologies were beginning to cast doubt on his thesis and more and more firms were starting to separate out many of their non-core activities. They found that any transaction costs were outweighed by the savings in overheads and fringe benefits that often go with membership of a large organisation. The loss of direct control was also counterbalanced by the psychological benefits of independence. Contracts and alliances are cheaper and often work better than ownership. The shamrock organisation had arrived (see Essay 8).

Britain's National Health Service is surely too big to be an integrated organisation à la Coase theory, with 1.3 million staff across a confusing miscellany of organisations. It is crying out for a federal approach, dividing it up by regions. That would allow each region to be judged on its success in improving the overall health of its citizens, thereby giving prevention as much importance as care and cure. Under the principles of federalism the centre would keep control of strategy, major investments and the appointment of key staff across the organisation. It would also monitor key results and cost but would not intervene to direct or control them except in extreme circumstances. In this way such a mammoth organisation might be brought down to a more human scale.

One aspect of the Second Curve has to be a new emphasis in business and government on becoming better without becoming bigger, by working together without controlling. Governments could go further in restricting the oligopolistic tendencies in particular industries. They could also use the tax regime to encourage smaller firms to remain in private ownership rather than running to the stock market as soon as they are viable, partly to enrich themselves. The banks might help, as they do in Germany, with longer-term loans in place of the short-term market-based financing that British and American bankers favour.

Those who favour bigger over better have to deal with one further question: is there ever such a thing as enough? When asked that question John D. Rockefeller is supposed to have answered 'Enough? Just one more!' Keynes disagreed. He believed that the economic problem would be solved in due course, in that all our physical needs would have been met, that three hours' work a day would be sufficient, leaving the big question of what we would do with all that leisure. We have thus far proved him wrong. Our needs, or more accurately our wants, have expanded as fast as our incomes. Logically there is no end to the growth of our appetites. In that sense Rockefeller was right. But so was Keynes.

If we cannot ever say to ourselves 'enough is enough' we will never be free to explore other possibilities. Keynes, therefore, was right in one sense, in that if we set a limit to our needs and wants, or to our hopes of success, we will have more time at our disposal. In the endless pursuit of more, whatever more is, we make ourselves slaves to our ambitions to which there is, in theory, no end. All political careers end in failure, it is said, unless one leaves before the end, calling it enough, and goes on to other things. A business cannot grow exponentially for ever. It becomes too big to manage satisfactorily, breaks itself up, or is broken up, reorganises and refocuses on new directions. It can be more satisfying, and often more profitable, to grow different rather than bigger. This is the premise behind the Second Curve, that different is more fruitful than more of the same.

The individual pursuit of more money is a particular snare, because there is no obvious end to it. There will always be someone with more to act as a comparison and a challenge. It is one of the paradoxes of growth that it can end up as a recipe for perpetual dissatisfaction. One solution is to say 'enough' and move on. Easy to say, hard to do. In our personal lives my wife and I set our own targets for the money that we need to earn each year and the time that we need to allocate to it. We have found that the lower we set the targets the more free we are to take up Keynes' challenge of how best to use the time we have released. Since the targets are made by us for us there is no envy of those who earn more or achieve more. Our life is more under our control than determined by some market. Those who choose to be poor are indeed blessed, with more freedom and opportunity to develop their own idea of success. Not so, of course, those who have poverty thrust upon them.

Growth, when one looks at it more closely, turns out to be a simplistic and confusing goal, one to be pursued with care and discretion. A society that believes that more is always better will be an envious and probably dissatisfied society. A society on a Second Curve would find better ways of measuring growth, recording its flaws as well as its successes, so that all that matters gets counted and included. A Second-Curve society would encourage the idea of enough, in order to curb unthinking consumerism and personal indebtedness. A Second Curve would also see the dismantling of some of the giants of business and finance into their component parts. Growth should always be the means to a greater purpose rather than an end in itself.

7

THE GLASS TOWERS OF CAPITALISM

Do we need a new capitalism?

WHERE WOULD WE be without capitalism and the free enterprise system? It has enriched the world hugely over the last three centuries and continues today to create wealth and work. You have to ask, however, as many now do, whether the wealth and work are as fairly distributed as they should be, whether the single-minded pursuit of wealth is not only leaching our societies but also putting power beyond the reach of the people and their politicians. Pope Francis, in his first encyclical in 2013, lamented the poison caused by the market economy that puts profit ahead of people. His lament is echoed by the protesters around the world, angered by the growing gap between the 1 per cent and the 99 per cent. We have to ask, has capitalism overreached itself? Can we put it back in its box without losing its vigour and creativity? Is it already too late?

Capitalism was given its huge boost by two creative social inventions back in the mid-19th century, when the twin ideas of the joint-stock company and limited liability were first widely applied in Britain. Their combination fuelled the Industrial Revolution by sharing and limiting the risk of investment. But down the centuries those good ideas have had some very unintended consequences, as good ideas often do. For a visible sign of the outcome of those social inventions one has only to look at the changing skylines of our cities, how the castles and cathedrals of the Middle Ages have been replaced, first by the parliaments of the people but now by the shining glass towers of the corporate world. To the average passer-by it seems clear where the real power now lies. What will the skylines look like in another hundred years, one wonders.

They are full of paradoxes, those towers. They are clothed in glass but you can't see into them. Proud symbols of successful democracies, they are as centrally controlled as any authoritarian regime. The names on their doors, often paraded on their rooftops, are, as often as not, a set of meaningless initials. To the layman, these are anonymous organisations, run by anonymous people, themselves the appointed agents of anonymous investors, represented, as often as not, by anonymous institutions in similar towers. You cannot blame that passer-by for thinking that power and wealth had somehow got out of his or her control, that their concerns and those of the wider society were in danger of being ignored. That is, if they thought about it at all. Perhaps the real problem is that too many people don't think that much about it, that they just assume it is the way it was ordained to be – just like slavery of old. That is not going to be the best starting point for a cultural change which, I will argue, is sorely needed, a Second Curve for capitalism.

It is now fashionable for some to prefer a campus to a tower, looking more like a university and sometimes structured like one as well. The office in one of the towers in which I once sat is now the living room of a smart apartment block. But even these campuses will be surrounded by high fences, with guards on the gates, still off-limits to the ordinary citizen, still mysterious, still answerable to no one save themselves and their invest- ors, their remuneration fixed by people like themselves, carefully keeping it just above the average, an average that therefore inexorably increases. The 'cui bono?' question – for whose benefit? – is still begging, with some seeing the answer to be only too obvious. To the passers-by, those towers or barricaded campuses do not seem to be working for anyone's good but their own. Ironically, that feeling is strongest in the developing world where the beneficial effects of capitalism are most needed. Of course, that is not the way all those mostly well-meaning people on the inside of those towers and campuses see it. They are just doing their best in a difficult world. That way delusion lies.

Henry Mintzberg, that scourge of the conventional in management thinking, has cogently argued that we took the wrong lesson from the collapse of the Soviet Union and the supposed 'triumph of capitalism'. It wasn't capitalism that brought it down, he suggests, but a society overbalanced by the state. Now the converse is true. The balance has swung the other way; society fetishises the private sector at the expense of government and the plural society. The result, paradoxically, is the same. He quotes the economist J. K. Galbraith: 'Under capitalism, man exploits man. Under communism it's just the opposite.'

Francis Fukuyama and others have argued, and many statesmen have assumed, that a combination of liberal democracy and open market capitalism would be the ultimate answer for a successful society. But democracy and capitalism can be uneasy bedfellows. If capitalism is not seen to be working for the demos the demos could destroy it, as the Occupy movement has sought to do. They, however, had no plausible alternative, no Second Curve, to propose, which suggests that protests alone won't kill capitalism. It is more likely that public pressure will end up by entangling business in so many restrictions and requirements that its vigour will be irreparably damaged. Some bankers fear that this is already happening in their bit of the world. We should have a care lest we kill the goose that lays the golden eggs. Revenge, if that is what it is, is a dish best served cold.

We do, therefore, urgently need a cultural shift in the way companies behave and in the way they are perceived in the wider society. It cannot be left to governments alone. In my experience, politicians do not move until they believe that their moves will be welcomed by a substantial section of the voting public. Which may take too long. Nor should we be tempted to discard those good ideas that have brought us so much good in the past. Companies are too precious to be lost to society. We have to ask, therefore, how did it get this way? How did such historically good ideas get corrupted? How can we rescue the good and eliminate the bad? There is a pile of good ideas already on the table. Transparency, accountability and governance structures are probably at the top of the list but I worry most about the big question that sits underneath these more technical issues. What is a business for, or even, perhaps, who is it for? More concretely, how should a business define success, and how measure it?

If one takes the trouble to look into company law it is clear that the corporation has much more freedom than some would previously have granted it to define its own destiny, and that there is a plethora of different models to choose from. Companies are not, as some assume, the vassals of their shareholders. A company is a legal person, in every country. The shareholders do not own the business, just the shares. There is a difference. The formal rights of those shareholders only extend to the appointment of a board, and to the remaining assets of the business on its break-up after all other claimants have been paid. The responsibilities of the directors are to the company as a whole, not to the shareholders alone. It was a widespread misinterpretation of company law that gave rise to the elevation of shareholder value as the prime purpose of the company, to short-term thinking and the splurge of bonuses tied to share performance.

As Jack Welch, the famed CEO of GE, was to remark, although only after he had left the firm, 'shareholder value is the dumbest idea in the world'. It may be a dumb idea but it was pervasive. In 1998 I was asked to meet with the committee that were updating the British Companies Act. I made them aware of what I felt was the true purpose of a company but they told me that they were under instructions from the Treasury to ensure that the shareholder must remain the central focus. Eventually they added the word 'enlightened' before 'shareholder value' and included a clause stating that the interests of other stakeholders must be recognised. Those were weasel words, easily ignored.

It is tempting to lay that fatal misinterpretation of company law at the door of two men, Michael Jensen and William H. Meckling, who published a paper in 1976 with the unexciting title of 'Theory of the Firm: Managerial Behavior, Agency Costs and Ownership Structure' in the then little-known *Journal of Financial Economics*, although the roots of their idea can be found in the thesis of their one-time colleague Milton Friedman who argued, famously, back in 1970 that 'the social responsibility of business is to increase its profits'. Set business free to do its job and all else would follow, he argued, society would grow and all would be better off. Jensen and Meckling's paper went on to be the most quoted economics article in the world for the next decade or two.

Jensen and Meckling argued that the firm was really a bundle of contractual relationships, that directors and managers were the agents of the owners and were not there for their own advantage. They advocated that directors and managers should align themselves with the shareholders, rewarding themselves as if they were shareholders with shares, stock options and bonuses tied to the performance of the shares. All this, incidentally, while still luxuriating in the security of their basic salaries. Naturally this focused managerial efforts on the immediate and shorter-term results, often at the expense of longer-term investments. To make matters worse, the business schools, which were just starting to proliferate around the world at that time, picked up the idea of shareholder value as the point of business and over the next 30 years disgorged a generation of bright and ambitious young people into corporations with this idea in their heads.

In 1971 I invited Jim Slater to speak to the students at the London Business School. Slater, as part of Slater Walker, was the uncrowned king of the emerging private equity industry. 'I am,' he said, 'the only businessman in Britain who does not make or do things for money. I am only interested in making money.' The students were fascinated, the rot had started and I was as guilty as anyone. As the seductive message spread, businesses no longer concentrated on making and doing things with profit as just one outcome, but focused exclusively on making money for the shareholders and, coincidentally, for themselves. Financiers replaced engineers at the head of manufacturing companies and the culture of corporations changed. They became, and still largely are, money-making machines. If indeed it be true that Jensen and Meckling's article started all this, it not only demonstrates the power of an idea to change the world, but also endorses Keynes' quip that 'Practical men, who believe themselves to be quite exempt from any intellectual influence, are usually the slaves of some defunct economist.'

It has taken 40 years for people to begin to see that Milton Friedman's idea was not working. Society has not benefited, indeed it almost collapsed in 2008, when banks and businesses overreached themselves. Most people in society are no better off in real terms than they were when he spoke, although 1 per cent are doing very nicely, thank you, and you can imagine who they are. Even the supposed beneficiaries of the theory, the shareholders, haven't benefited. The distinguished academic Roger Martin has calculated that, overall, company profits were lower in the 40 years after 1970 than they were in the 40 years before, when managers were paid normal salaries to do their job. If we seem to be living better lives it is mainly because there are now two earners in each family where one used to suffice, and those two are working harder and longer than ever before. That is not the way the world was meant to be.

Unfortunately the inhabitants of the glass towers still sit in their own worlds above the rest of us. Take the recent rise in share buybacks in the USA; Professor William Lazonick has calculated that the 449 quoted companies in the S&P 500 index that were publicly listed from 2003 to 2012 used 54 per cent of their earnings, a grand total of $2.4 trillion, to buy back their own stock. Given that dividends take up another 37 per cent of those earnings, companies are left with a meagre 9 per cent for reinvestment. Companies buy back their own shares when they have, in theory, more money than they need to ensure their future. Buying back their own shares means fewer shares sharing the same profits. That then pushes up the share price and the return on equity. Very nice for those at the top whose pay is increasingly designed to reflect the share price, with stock grants and options, in the USA, accounting for 80 per cent of their total remuneration; not so nice for the rest of us who might prefer to see that money invested in new products, better training or even better wages and salaries for the less senior employees. It gets even stranger when companies such as Apple, who pile up their profits overseas to save tax, find it pays them to borrow tax-deductible money at home to buy back their own shares, leaving the profits safely offshore. Of course there are deviations from this theme. Not all boards are so self-interested, but the exceptions are just that – exceptions.

William Lazonick comments that from the end of the First World War until the late seventies the prevailing orthodoxy in the boardrooms of the world was to 'retain and reinvest' one's earnings. Now it is to 'downsize and distribute', to ourselves and our supportive shareholders. We have moved from value creation to value extraction. He is right. When I started work in 1956 in the Royal Dutch Shell Group I remember only too well the opening briefing that we fledgling executives received from one of the managing directors in our first week of training: 'We are,' he said, 'an important part of the energy supply system of the world. Our job is to supply our customers with their needs and to secure the long-term future of the business. We need to make substantial profit in order to finance that future. We also pay a rent to our shareholders, in the form of dividends, for the use of their money, a rent that includes a risk premium, although in our case that premium is low and we want to keep it that way.' I wonder if he would say the same today.

Those at the top of the glass towers must believe that their skills and talents justify their rewards. The Greeks of old would have called that hubris, which I was taught to translate as overweening pride, that which comes before a fall. The basic facts suggest that the corporate fall may be nearer than we know. A recent Brookings Institution research report found that firms aged 16 or older now represented 34 per cent of all economic activity in the USA, up 50 per cent in

20 years. They are also not lasting as long with fewer new entrants coming along, which bodes ill for the future. There are now 50 per cent fewer publicly listed companies in America than there were 15 years ago; nor is it very different in the rest of the world. Businesses, at least in America, the Brookings report concludes, are getting older, fatter and fewer. That should concern us all.

Can we safely trust these big, ageing, bloated and selfish organisations with our futures? Is it not time to return to the idea of a business as a responsible community that pays due heed to all its constituents, one whose core purpose must be to seek immortality through continuous self-improvement and investment? I have concentrated on America, where corporate capitalism has been most developed, but the same trend is discernible in other economies. Continental Europe is protected to a degree by its more rigorous governance structures and its greater reliance on the banks as the longer-term financiers, but even here the temptations and pressures of the shareholder value model can be felt.

We have got the idea of a company the wrong way round. It is not a creation of shareholders, creditors and directors but an association of all those working in and with it. It is a community, a collection of people working together for a common purpose. It is strange that the one area of human life which is so important to our well-being, that of business, still legally treats its people as instruments of a money-making property.

It is time that those 'instruments' were enfranchised, both for their own sake and for the health of the organisation. Free people do not relish being the instruments of others. The best of them will, increasingly, either refuse to join such institutions or demand a high price for the sacrifice of their rights. A gentleman, said Confucius, is not an instrument. In 1891 Pope Leo XIII, in his encyclical *Rerum Novarum* on the 'Rights and Duties of Capital and Labour', said, 'To misuse men as though they were things in the pursuit of gain . . . is truly shameful and inhuman.' Few were listening. Worse, many were only too happy to collude in this form of voluntary servitude. More than 120 years later it is time that we finally paid attention.

It is interesting to consider the implications that would follow if we thought of a business as a community rather than a property. No one can own a community, although they can help to finance it and can have a stake in it. Its members, in turn, belong to it but are not owned by it. As the word 'company' suggests, they are companions and are more properly regarded as citizens than as employees or 'human resources', citizens with responsibilities as well as rights, someone whose interests are intimately tied up with those of the corporation as a whole, or at least of their particular operating unit. The board of the corporation can then be held accountable for the company and its future to all its citizens and all its interest groups, be they inside or outside the company, not just to its financiers. That would bring it back into line with the proper interpretation of company law. It would make it a more natural fit with a democratic society.

The proper responsibility of a business community, surely, is to create wealth for society as a whole, to produce the goods and services that their customers need and want, to provide employment and a way of life for those who work in them, all at fair prices, and to do no harm to the environment around them – in other words to do their job in the best possible way for the benefit not of themselves alone but of all their stake-holders, and to continue to do so for as long as possible.

If we are not all going to be forced to be mercen-aries, on sale to the highest bidder, hired for projects, unwanted when not needed, loyal first to ourselves, then to our project and only last and least to the hiring organisation, then we shall have to cultivate the culture of citizenship and all that it involves. The cultural change that this would involve would be the Second Curve that capitalism so badly needs. Some might say that this is just semantic quibbling, but words matter, they are the clues to meaning. Change the words and you begin to change the way you think. That in turn changes the way you behave.

What would a company of citizens look like? In what ways would it be different? These questions are dealt with in the next essay.

8

THE CITIZEN ORGANISATION

Should organisations be more democratic?

'WHY CAN'T THEY be more like us?' The speaker was the vice-chancellor of a university. She was responding to my observation that most large businesses seem to be more like the totalitarian centrally planned regimes of the old communist world than anything resembling democracy. That communist world was brought down by its bureaucratic rigidity and by its inability to harness the energies and enthusiasm of its people in pursuit of its cause. That fate, I was suggesting, may yet await the corporations of the West unless they can find a better way to involve those who work there in the governance and management of the organisation to which they belong. After all, as I said in the last essay, calling it a company suggests that there should be companions, not just employees.

My university friend had a point, although when I suggested it to a senior executive of a business his response was 'Then God help us all', which only demonstrates how far off the prospect of business democracy is. But I was serious. Universities have things to teach business, just as business has some things to teach them. Universities are storehouses of human intellectual property. They have to treat their key staff as members, not employees, individuals who collectively resource and run the institution. They are effectively self-governing and owned by no one, even if funded largely by the state. They set their own goals and measure their own outcomes, responsible only to themselves, their students and their vision. They are mutual organisations, although they never call themselves that. Businesses these days are no different, although they would not admit it. Their employees may be their principal assets but that does not mean that they are just human resources (a depressing term) to be used as and when needed. They are individuals, citizens not subjects, and deserve to be treated as such.

Democracy is forced upon the organisation of a university. Its key members, the faculty, are keenly aware that they are the only real assets of the organisation and that the organisation does not have the resources to buy out their democratic rights, much as it would like to on occasion. Bizarrely, perhaps, there is a model for the way they are constructed. It can be found the city state of Athens in its heyday, supposedly the prototype of democracy, a place where the people thought of themselves as citizens, not subjects, from its earliest times. Although it is rash to think that we can copy history there are things that we can learn from models of the past. Consider the facts, to start with. During the nearly 200 years of its independent existence – a lifespan that most organisations can only dream of – the Athenians fought and won major wars, built and lost an empire, suffered defeats and confronted organisational crises, but their self-governing democracy allowed them to bounce back time and again to recover their prosperity and expand their reputation for innovation and culture. We still remember their organisation, which is more than can be said of any of the business empires of yesteryear.

Citizenship in universities, as in Athens of old, is restricted. In the case of Athens it was granted only to locally born males with property. Tenure in universities is the mark of full citizenship but only those who are judged to merit it are awarded it. In which case they become citizens for life and, in return for this privilege, they are expected to have a regard for the university as well as for themselves – that paradox of citizenship that requires one to balance self-interest with a contribution to the community. Each citizen typically belongs, as in Athens, to a smaller group, or department, as well as to the greater body of the faculty. Major decisions are ratified by a meeting of the whole citizen body, normally known as the Senate, which acts as the legislative chamber, akin to the Assembly of Athens which all citizens were entitled to attend, although most seldom bothered. A smaller executive body manages the day-to-day affairs. Management roles are usually rotated, as in Athens, with deans or heads of departments serving for fixed terms before reverting to their academic tasks. There are other paid staff who are not faculty and who don't get to vote. Perhaps they should, for otherwise they are the equivalent of the women of Athens, who probably had their say back home but not in public, or even of the helots and slaves who had no rights at all in Athens.

The result is not always the harmonious efficiency that was hoped for. Decision-making can be slow and ponderous, although not necessarily worse in its final outcomes; personal agendas can obstruct progress; small groups can dampen initiative as well as encourage it, while the security of citizenship can breed caution and conservatism rather than brave new visions, as it did in Athens towards the end. Equally, overconfidence in an assembly can lead to vainglorious adventures or strategic overreach, like the Athenians' doomed Sicilian adventure in the Peloponnesian War. Paradoxically, perhaps, democracies need strong leadership in order to function well. Athens was at its best when people such as Cleisthenes or Pericles were at its head, men who had both vision and the ability to persuade rather than command their fellow citizens.

So it is in universities. Only a strong and well-accepted leader can rally the citizens to a common cause, one that overrides personal or group agendas, one that will persuade people to sacrifice something for the common good. Otherwise frustration at inaction can lead to breakaway factions and, as in Athens, attempted coups. Athens never found her Second Curve after her defeat by the Spartans and went into a long and slow decline, but her model of participative citizenship lasted for over 200 years. Many universities can equal or even far exceed that record, which is not bad compared with the shelf life of most publicly owned companies, currently around 14 years, as noted in the first essay.

The Athenian model of a self-governing state is impressive, but a university, let alone a corporation, is not a state. A university cannot embrace the whole life of its workers, nor do they necessarily expect to live and work in it for ever, or even for long. They can expect to survive even if the organisation collapses. Their commitment and involvement is correspondingly less. This is particularly so when the organisation is supposedly owned by outsiders whose duty of care to those who work in it is heavily circumscribed by the desire, and the supposed legal obligation in many countries, to look after their own interests first. Nevertheless, the ideas that helped Athens to flourish and to survive the vicissitudes of 200 years do have relevance to the corporate communities of the modern world.

Voluntary societies are more citizen-friendly than many businesses. As with the universities, their citizens are their key assets and understandably like to be involved in all decisions. They have constitutions with elected assembles or councils to whom they are responsible, sitting on top of management boards. To them it is plain that their clients or customers come first and that the finances of the organisation are the means not the end. That is clear from their annual reports, which start by recording how well they have carried out their responsibilities to their clients or their cause, with finances relegated to the back of the report. It is typically the other way round in company reports: money results come first, customers and workers second.

Businesses have, with some justification, shied away from the participative model of the university, believing it to be too slow and cumbersome. Nevertheless, they still have to deal with the increasingly vociferous demands of their principal assets, their citizens. Those that can afford it have, in effect, bought out the citizenship rights of their key people with enhanced salaries, bonuses and stock options, bribing them into acquiescence with their rulers, content, for a price, to be subjects not citizens. This mercenary option can be prohibitively expensive and often short-term at best as those human assets continue to raise their price or go elsewhere. Like it or not, businesses and indeed other organisations will have to find ways to incorporate the ideas of citizenship without sacrificing either efficiency or strategic vision.

To get them thinking, all they need to do is to look at some recent findings on the levels of engagement by the workforce in large organisations. The evidence is disturbing: 80 per cent of them say they are not really engaged with the work of the organisation. As one

French CEO put it, 'They only turn up to go home,' being only there for their pay. Worse, one-quarter of that 80 per cent are actively disengaged and would be prepared to activate their latent negative power to disrupt the work if provoked. A mere 20 per cent are actively involved and committed to the work, with some surveys putting the figure as low as 13 per cent. That so many of the rest should spend such a large part of their waking hours going through the motions is sad beyond belief. We need to rethink the way we design our organisations, if only to give the people in them more involvement in their work. An active citizenship, working within a democratic structure, is the sort of new curve that is needed. Some see the first signs of it in the rise of the mutuals which, in Britain, are growing at the rate of 9 per cent a year and outperforming traditional externally owned companies by 7 per cent. Mutuals, however, although important trailblazers, are but one form of a citizenship organisation.

The real way forward lies, perhaps, not in trying to emulate in any detail the practices of the universities or of ancient Athenians but to tease out the possibilities inherent in the use of a more political view of organisations. They could, for instance, explore the rights that citizenship confers, as a way of bonding the individual more securely to the organisation. This is the route followed by the social legislation of the European Union, which has introduced statutory rights for workers in all medium and large organisations.

These include minimum vacation periods, parental leave, the right of appeal against unfair dismissal and, in some circumstances, the right to be informed and consulted on major decisions that affect one's employment. Some organisations go further, practising what they call 'open-book management' in which all information is made available to all members of the organisation, with help offered for its interpretation. As in Athens, transparency is seen as a way of building confidence and trust.

A step more would be to give tenured workers, those on so-called 'indefinite period contracts', the same right to vote as shareholders. A fixed proportion of votes, perhaps in the form of non-tradable but voting shares, could be allocated to the workers, giving them an effective say in key decisions. Alternatively, key decisions could be required to be ratified by a majority of the tenured workforce. This might not be so cumbersome as it sounds if the current trends in the workplace continue. In the interests of flexibility and reducing costs, organisations are putting on the outside every activity that is not vital to their identity. If someone can do something better than you they should be paid to do it for you, as long as they are not on your payroll or premises, be it the catering, the management of the site, the accounting, the computing or even the human resource department. That leaves the organisation with its key workers, those who can rightly be called its members or its citizens, leaving outside the semi-detached workers as the equivalent of the helots or the women in ancient Athens, necessary but not included.

There are businesses who do even more, giving their real shares to their workers, creating an employee-owned organisation like John Lewis in Britain, in which the shares pay out what is effectively an annual dividend although they cannot be sold. Others put employee shares into a trust which pays dividends but provides no individual voting rights. Others can go further still and give the shares to their customers, as the traditional building societies did. On balance, a compromise is needed between the need for involvement and the need for effective management, resulting in the limited citizenship outlined above.

I have in the past called this emerging organisational form a 'shamrock organisation'.

A shamrock, like a clover, has only three leaves. In my concept the first, central leaf is made up of the core workforce, who together own the key intellectual and management skills of the organisation, the things that make it what it is, what the management thinkers Gary Hamel and the late C. K. Prahalad have called its core competence. In the second leaf are the secondary organisations to which some of the subsidiary work of the organisation is outsourced. The third leaf is a combination of hired individuals, some of them highly skilled but too expensive to be employed full-time, some of them lower-skilled part-time help. The stalk of the leaf is the management that holds it all together. The exact balance between the three leaves depends on the needs and situation of each organisation. A university is heavily dependent on the central leaf. Many a small consultancy will operate with a minute centre and a band of free associates in the third leaf. Some organisations go too far and put too many of their functions in the second leaf, thereby losing control of some key aspects of their work.

In the citizenship model only those in the central leaf would be given citizenship, with all its rights and responsibilities. The precise shape and balance of the shamrock is therefore a key decision for any organisation, be it a university, a voluntary organisation or a commercial concern. They cannot afford to be too generous with the rights of citizenship, but they need the commitment that comes with it. Universities typically wait until someone has proved themselves before they award them tenure and a permanent contract. A key question for a business shamrock is the position of the shareholders. They are not, and cannot be, a part of the shamrock. Stretching the metaphor a bit, they are best seen as the fertiliser or the planter of the seed, crucial but outside, investors not partners. As investors they currently have the sole right to elect the directors of the company. In a citizenship business they will have to share these rights with the citizen body. They will naturally resist, but, in time, they will have to accept that those who provide their knowledge, skills and energies have as much right to influence the policy of the organisation as those who have loaned it their money or, in most cases, merely traded in its shares.

Citizenship is the key concept in a democracy. Odd then that Britain still calls its people subjects not citizens. Maybe its organisations will be the first to give the idea its proper prominence, if only to secure their survival in a mercenary world. If they do they will be working with the grain of the new workforce which is growing up influenced by the new shape of the home and family that has come about in the last 30 years or so. Michael Maccoby, a psychoanalyst and renowned leadership authority, has described how the modern dual-career or single-parent families, with children in day care from their early years, have created young adults with a more interactive social character and disposition. They have learnt to depend more on their peer group than their parents, while their confident access to every kind of information makes them more ready to challenge authority, to be free agents in charge of their own lives.

Such people, Maccoby says, are used to shared leadership and, having been brought up to regard their parents as service providers rather than authority figures, have learnt negotiating skills early on. As a result they have no problems in questioning or contradicting authority. Having acquired interactive skills in their early schooling, they like working in groups, solving problems and developing these skills. As a consequence of their upbringing, they have learnt only to respect leaders who respect them. Often knowing more about their jobs than their bosses and adept at using social and information technologies, they can be demanding but interesting colleagues. In short, they see themselves very much as independent citizens not as subjects and will not adapt readily to the imposed authority of a more bureaucratic regime. While this may not be true of all of the rising generation, it does describe the kind of talented self-confident individuals we might expect to find in the core leaf of the shamrock, the ones who are vital to the future of the organisation. These are also the sort of people who would value and profit from a citizen company.

In spite of all this, left to themselves corporations are unlikely to adopt any form of the citizenship model because they fear the loss of control that it implies. The danger is that they will leave it too late to change their minds, until the curve has long since peaked and they find themselves struggling with a reluctant workforce and declining profitability. The past is once again the obstacle to a new vision of the corporation. The change will come, if it does, from new organisations led by individuals of the sort that Maccoby envisages, who will want to create the kind of company that they themselves would be comfortable working for, because a Second Curve in organisations or society is seldom led by those who were in charge of the first curve. Sad but true.

9

THE NEW MANAGEMENT

Why is it needed? What is it?

WALKING THROUGH ONE of London's largest department stores I paused in the middle of the linen section. I looked at the seemingly endless piles of towels, sheets, duvet covers, you name it, in every conceivable size and colour. How had they all got here? Who had ordered them, decided on the range, the numbers, the sizes? Who had got them delivered, priced them and put them on the racks? Well, lots of different people, of course, most of whom did not know each other. It was, in short, the outcome of a well-designed management system that made it possible for disparate groups of people to do together what they could not conceivably do on their own. Rather magical, when you think about it, although we don't much, taking it all for granted. Yet we see that magic replicated every day wherever we look, in the trains and planes we travel on, the programmes we watch on the television, the oil we use and the food we buy. Unseen and unnoticed, all the relevant bits are brought together to give us what we need or want. The magic does not always work as well as it should, but that it works as well as it does most of the time is still remarkable.

Which is why management, an ugly word for that bit of magic, is crucial to a modern economy. Big organisations depend on it. We all do, as customers. Peter Drucker, the uber-guru of management, called it society's unseen central resource that made the 20th century possible. We live in an organisational economy, as he pointed out, one still dominated by the large elephants of commerce in which most of us work. So, if management is so important and, at its best, almost miraculous in what it achieves, why does it have such a bad reputation in so many quarters? To quote Drucker again, why does 'so much of management [consist] of making it difficult for people to work'? Why too, asks the journalist Simon Caulkin, are managers 'still building mass-production organisations fit for the early 20th century, based on hierarchy, standardisation and compliance, rather than flexible, human-centred outfits in which technology is not a threat but a partner of both employees and customers'? That old idea of what management is and how it works has reached the end of the road. Mass-production organisations look good on the drawing board but not in the real world as it is today. They are too expensive, too draining to work in, too cumbersome, too complicated and, often, too big. At their heart is a set of confusions. We need, I believe, a Second Curve of management thinking that resolves these confusions and provides a new model.

The first confusion is the familiar one between management and leadership. Management may be the glue that holds society and organisations together but it is leadership that decides where they are going and ensures that there are those who will accompany them. The late Warren Bennis, my valued mentor and a long-term student of leadership, said, 'Managers do things right, leaders do the right things.' I would add another distinction: management is a word that we properly use to describe the organisation of things or systems; leadership is the word that we ought to use when we refer to people. If you think about it, those organisations where people have always been their main or only resource, such as universities and professional bodies, tend to use words like Principal, Dean, Partner or, once in my case, Warden for their senior positions, reserving Manager for areas such as catering, transport or facilities, where the system is the key element.

Once again, the words we use shape the way we think. Management language is that of engineering. It sees people as human resources to be utilised, and the organisation as a machine that can be fine-tuned, controlled and directed. No one, however, likes to think of themselves being managed, but they seldom feel it undignified to be led. That is because leadership recognises that people are individuals with minds of their own who have to be persuaded, inspired and cajoled. Leadership talks of vision, mission and passion, management of targets, controls and efficiency. Management relies on what is termed position power, the authority of office, leadership on earned authority, given to one by the people involved.

Every organisation needs both, but each in its right place. Too much management and too little leadership creates the kind of organisational anomie that the surveys throw up. On the other hand, the systems on which the organisation runs need to be well designed and managed. To work effectively those well-designed management systems need leadership within them, to provide the heart and the energy. Too often, unfortunately, the demands of the bureaucracy are so dominant that the leadership requirement gets neglected. We don't, for instance, talk of leading a bureaucracy or a system, yet it cannot be emphasised enough that organisations are communities not machines. Machines need management. Communities need leaders, supported by management.

The political historian Giles Radice, in his recent book *Odd Couples*, examines the often odd couples whom history threw together at various times to run the country. The first couple he looks at is Churchill and Attlee, who together headed the grand coalition that governed Britain during the Second World War. Each needed the other: Churchill was the great persuader and visionary, Attlee was the implementer and enabler, a gifted chairman. Churchill was clearly the leader, but a leader without a manager is futile. Attlee built and maintained the systems that kept the country running. In that sense he was the manager.

Asked once what Churchill did to help win the war, Attlee said, 'He talked about it,' which, of course, he did to great effect. Interestingly, when Attlee became Prime Minister after the war he maintained his implementing managerial role, allowing the big beasts in his cabinet, Bevin, Bevan and Morrison, to do the persuading, the leadership role. Wise are they who know their own talents and limitations, for few can be both leader and manager, yet both are essential. Too often the successful manager, in both politics and business, is promoted to the leadership role only to find that the attention to systems and detail that served so well in the past are no substitute for the visionary and persuasive skills of leadership that are now needed.

A leader without the backup of an implementer is also likely to fail. I shall always remember the great walk that a friend arranged to celebrate his big birthday. We divided into two groups and agreed to meet up in a distant village for lunch. 'I know the way,' said a member of our group, a distinguished ambassador, 'follow me.' He strode off while we were still talking among ourselves. When we looked up he had disappeared into the woodland. We never saw him again. He needed someone to round us up, to organise us, an implementer. Leaders without followers are not much use.

Too many books have been written about leadership and what it involves for the advice they give to need repeating here. They could all be summed up for me by the recommendation I once heard given to a would-be leader: 'Know yourself, know where you want to go, know your people, be humble and listen.' Everything else then falls into place. The wise words of John Garnett when director of the Industrial Society in London also ring in my ears whenever the issue of leadership crops up: 'If you care about what they care about, they'll care about what you care about.' Obvious really, but easier to say than to do. Some have a flair for leadership but can sometimes be carried away by their own enthusiasms, as Churchill arguably was on occasion, but the best leaders grow into it or rise to the occasion. Some are noisy and exuberant, out in front; others are quiet team builders. Just don't expect any of them to be managers as well.

The second confusion is that between trust and control. Trust is cheaper but control is safer, or so we think. I once worked with a colleague who specialised in team management, how to get groups to work together more effectively. He left to go and fulfil a long-time dream, to open a restaurant. I met him a year or so later. 'It must be nice,' I said, 'to be able to put all your ideas into practice in your own establishment.' 'It's funny,' he replied, 'but I haven't actually used any of that stuff. I found that if you get the right people to start with and they know what to do then they get on with it by themselves.' Jim Collins, in his book *Good to Great*, found that successful companies 'paid scant attention to managing change, motivating people or creating alignment'; they didn't need to because their people knew what they were doing and wanted to do it well. You could call it managing without managers.

I was lucky; my first proper job with Royal Dutch Shell was as the manager in charge of their marketing company in Sarawak, a Bornean state the size of England, albeit one with only 30 miles of tarred roads. I was 25 years old and knew very little about management or oil or marketing or Sarawak. I had a lot to learn. The year was 1958 and communications between my office in Kuching, the capital, and headquarters in Singapore were non-existent. Mail took the best part of a week to get through and my superiors seldom visited. They had no alternative but to trust me. That was frightening at first, with no one to turn to, but I discovered one advantage as I began to make mistake after mistake: I was able to correct each mistake as soon as I became aware of it and before anyone back in headquarters knew about it. I learnt fast, soon began delivering on time and on budget, and had an unblemished record as far as they knew. Had they been able to monitor me more closely I would no doubt have been not just reprimanded but possibly recalled. Their trust in me was risky but cheaper and, for me, infinitely more exciting and rewarding.

Modern information systems have the dubious advantage of being potentially real-time and all-encompassing, meaning that someone can keep a close tab on all details of every bit of the operation. Used indiscriminately this can inhibit initiative and breed resentment and distrust.

One estimate suggested that 27 million employees world-wide had their internet usage monitored. No one wants someone looking over their shoulder all the time. Surround people with too many rules and regulations and they stop thinking for themselves. If it is allowed it must be OK, is a way of thinking that led many bankers to behave legally but irresponsibly in the past. I liked the department store that I came across in which every sales assistant carried a card in their breast pocket with the company rule on it. It read: 'Do whatever you think is right.' The implications of that simple statement for the recruitment and training in that store are worth thinking about. Trust does not come free. On the other hand control systems and the checkers that come with them also cost money. Used carefully, and designed only to throw up anomalies, automatic information systems can be a reassuring tool for management, but one has to beware of the temptation to use something just because it is available.

The third confusion is the difference between effi-ciency and effectiveness. They should be the same but, in practice, they work differently. Efficiency starts from the input end while effectiveness works back from the end results. As Peter Drucker also said, 'There is nothing quite so useless as doing with great efficiency something that should not be done at all.' Or the opposite, I would add, not doing what should be done because it would cost more, and therefore would appear to be less efficient. Required to increase efficiency, the prison service in Britain was asked to cut costs. They therefore sliced off what they saw as non-essential activities in order to keep security at the necessary level. The problem, as the journalist and blogger Simon Caulkin pointed out, was that these non-essentials included such things as education and gardening which had proved to be the most effective ways of preventing reoffending after leaving prison. In other words, the efficiency savings resulted in more returning prisoners, thus increasing the cost in the long run. Had they started at the other end, with the evidence of the relative longer-term effectiveness of different aspects of the prison regime, they might have decided differently.

The understandable desire for increased efficiency leads organisations to tighten things up and to cut costs. That leaves less room for unplanned or uncoordinated action. The result is to curb initiative if individuals or groups find that they cannot move without prior permission. This leads to confusion. The centre worries about the loss of momentum and is tempted to increase control, to centralise more. The individual units resent being curbed and give up trying. Efficiency then becomes the enemy of creativity, just when you need more and better ideas. The pressures for efficiency also lead to the temptations of reductionism, the idea that the whole is only the sum of its parts and that by breaking a system down into its separate bits and optimising those you will get the best result overall. The result can be a complicated web of interlocking departments and an inevitable increase in the transaction time and cost. Reductionism may work in engineering, but in organisations it is a dangerous fallacy. Try to get your proposal checked off by the 12 different departments involved if you want to test this out.

To those frustrated by the conflict between efficiency and effectiveness I would recommend some doughnut thinking. All jobs and team projects are, I suggest, doughnut-shaped.

The doughnut is an English doughnut, the kind with jam in the middle. The jam represents the core essentials of the job that is required of the person or the group. If they are not delivered you or your group will have failed. But there is more to the job than the specified core, there is the dough around the jam, the empty space for new initiatives. Efficiency dislikes empty space so is tempted to prescribe what should happen in it, thereby pulling more into the core. In the extreme all the doughnut is core, every action is foreseen and prescribed, as is the case in many call centres where the operator is totally constrained by what they read on their screen. The next stage is to do away with the operator and leave it to the computer, thereby giving complete control to the centre but also ensuring that no unexpected or creative initiatives will be forth-coming. Efficiency will have killed individual creativity and initiative.

The preferred solution is a compromise. The centre has control over the core of the work and can, by drawing the outer rim of the doughnut a bit tighter, limit the scope for initiative, while still leaving the individual or group room to be creative. How, then, does the organisation ensure that any initiatives will be in line with the organisation's purposes? Only by trusting that the individual or group has an understanding of those purposes and the accompanying values, to know instinctively what is the right thing to do. For that to happen, as I hinted earlier, the leadership has to ensure that their purposes, goals, values and criteria for success are well understood and that all necessary information on costs and profitability are made available to those involved. It is also rather important to ensure that the individual or group has the necessary competences to fill the doughnut and that their past record provides evidence that they are trustworthy. Doughnut management requires a major investment in the development of the staff. That may be expensive in the short term but, ultimately, trust is always cheaper than control. In a doughnut culture people are judged on the results, not on their methods, on their effectiveness rather than their efficiency. Efficiency should be the servant not the master.

The new technologies can now work both ways. Technology can be used, as in some of those call centres, to eliminate discretion and increase control, or, by monitoring only results and by more disclosure of necessary data, it can facilitate individual initiative. Some business organisations take the doughnut model to extremes, effectively licensing individual units to run their own businesses, or to start new ones, for which they would need corporate approval if investment were needed. Companies such as W. L. Gore and Semco have been going this way for years but, more recently, Haier in China, a huge domestic appliance firm, made it the heart of their organisational philosophy. Zhang Ruimin, the founder and boss, started dismantling the corporate hierarchy in 2009 and now has 2,000 self-managed teams. Any employee can generate their own new idea – for a new appliance model or a new feature on an existing model – by examining customer comments and market information. If approved by management that employee can create and manage their own team to implement the project, which will involve persuading specialist staff to contribute their time. Team members get a share in the resulting profits. In 2013 Zhang got rid of 16,000 staff from the old hierarchy. Now he and a small group of top executives keep a close eye on what is, in effect, a federation of tiny businesses – or doughnuts. More Chinese companies, it seems, are going the doughnut way, often allowing numbers of innovation projects to compete for customers, thus pulling in the customer to the innovation process. On a larger scale, Warren

Buffett, that master of the common-sense approach to business, runs his company, Berkshire Hathaway, with only 25 people at headquarters, overseeing around 80 separate companies with some 302,000 employees altogether. There are some big doughnuts there, but the principle is still the same, managing by trust and outcome, not control and process.

Doughnuts also help to resolve another confusion, that between allocation and delegation. Allocating particular tasks to someone and supervising their delivery is not proper delegation. Delegation is handing over responsibility for an area of work, leaving the process to be determined by the people involved – a whole doughnut, in other words, where the core specifies what has to be done but with space left for deciding on the best way to do it. It can be very frustrating to think you have been handed responsibility for something only to find that it was more truthfully an allocated task, or a doughnut that was all core.

Doughnuts work on trust and mutual cooperation. That puts a limit on their size because you cannot trust or rely on people that you do not know or may never have met. How big then is big? Robin Dunbar of Oxford University came up with a number. After examining studies of village communities and army units going back over time Dunbar suggested that one individual can only keep track of around 150 people at any one time. More recent evidence from Facebook communities supports this number, which would, I suggest, provide the maximum size for a doughnut, although smaller is always easier. Leadership, I have argued, means knowing your followers. You can't do that if there are too many people involved, too many therefore to know well enough to trust. Doughnut design is an essential part of a good management system while doughnut leadership is crucial to its effectiveness. The organisation of the British army is based on doughnuts. An infantry battalion has at its base platoons of three sections of eight persons. The platoon commander is expected to know all the soldiers in his platoon well enough to be able to rely upon them in combat situations. It is an organisational arrangement that has proved successful in a wide variety of situations down the years, even as the technology involved has changed radically.

Organisations of all sorts have become increasingly complex and confusing over time, as they look for economies of scale and for control through ever more complex systems, convoluted hierarchies and multiple coordinating groups. Most of the time any efficiencies gained are more than outweighed by the loss of enthusiasm, energy and initiative in the workforce. It is time to junk the old ideas and start a second simpler curve of thinking about the way to organise work and workplaces. In the end, I believe, good management is only common sense at heart, just not in common use. Add in an interest in those you work with, some decent humility, a will to listen and a desire to see a job well done and you have leadership theory in a nutshell. I call it the doughnut idea because I believe that images often speak louder than words, are more memorable and less threatening. Doughnuts are everyday common-place objects, as management ought to be.

10

THE PONZI SOCIETY

Are we drowning in debt? What are the consequences?

IN HIS NOVEL *Martin Chuzzlewit*, Charles Dickens
tells how Montague Tigg starts an insurance company
with no funds at all. The Anglo-Bengalee Loan and
Life Assurance Company paid out the claims of the
early policyholders from the premiums coming in from
later entrants. It is not known whether Charles Ponzi
in the United States read Dickens but his own scheme,
based on the arbitrage of international reply coupons,
followed the same principle, diverting any new income
to the early investors and to himself. When the scam
collapsed in 1920 the sums involved were so large that
Ponzi has given his name to all subsequent schemes.
More recently Bernard Madoff ran something very
similar, an investment fund that promised, and delivered, unusually high returns to investors for almost
50 years. When he was finally exposed, by his two sons,
his liabilities were, he admitted, around $50 billion,
although his early clients lost no money. He is currently
serving a sentence of 150 years.

How odd then that what was called the fraud of the century should be the common practice in much of society today. Take the state pension scheme in Britain for example. The state pension scheme in Britain is unfunded, as it is in most countries. That was not the original intention. Back in 1942 William Beveridge had wanted a contributory scheme, with people getting back at the end what they had put in. But it was soon obvious that the start-up would leave existing pensioners in the cold. So it was quickly changed to a pay-as-you-go system, similar to the way pensions are paid in most other countries, with provisos that required you to have paid contributions for specified periods of time.

The pensions are now paid out of current income, notionally from the contributions made by the recipients over their lifetime, but in reality from the contributions paid by those still earning, from the National Insurance levies and from general taxation. It is a bit deceptive since many who pay their National Insurance often believe that they are contributing to a pot that will in due course pay for their retirement and any unemployment, when in fact their contributions are paying for those who have gone before them and they will in turn be funded by those who come after.

This works well as long as there are more joining the workforce than leaving it, Ponzi-like, and ideally very many more because that keeps the cost down. The equation begins to falter if the numbers change and if people live longer. In years gone by there were six people in work for every one retired, and those often died in their seventies. What happens when there are only two workers for every pensioner and those pensioners live until they are nearly 90, as will be the case in Europe by 2050? When Ponzi schemes become unbalanced it is bad news for all involved. Already the income collected from National Insurance contributions in Britain is £10 billion less than the outgoings. It would be more honest and straightforward if the pretence of National Insurance were dropped and everything incorporated in general taxation.

It is just as bad at the personal level. Personal debt levels in Britain are running at £1.4 trillion, having doubled in the last decade, or £54,000 per household. Those figures include mortgages but there is still £95 billion owing to credit cards and other sources of financial credit. Interestingly, only 18 per cent thought that this was a heavy burden. Too many are happily living a Ponzi life, paying today's expenditure with tomorrow's money, and will come to rue it when their incomes sag or the cost of credit rises and mortgages become expensive once again. These debts are making a nonsense of much of the welfare system at the poorer levels of society where half of the benefits paid out can go straight away to pay the interest on payday loans, with not enough left over to live on, let alone pay off the original loan. It can be a trap for life.

Businesses will tell you that credit, or gearing as they call it, is no bad thing in moderation. It allows you to grow without waiting for your savings to accumulate. Gearing is only a fancy term for 'buy now pay later'. That works as long as the extra profit exceeds the cost of the credit plus the repayment. Our family rule is that it is prudent to borrow to invest but not to consume; in other words, mortgages are good in moderation but credit-card balances and overdrafts can be bottomless pits. It is no different in government. A deficit is like an overdraft, sensible only in the short term. A debt incurred to finance an asset is like a mortgage, an investment in the future. Governments can legitimately borrow to invest, even if it increases the national debt, provided that the benefit ultimately justifies the cost, but they should beware of allowing the deficit, the national overdraft, to grow too far, allowing for the fact that increasing the debt also increases the interest payments. Best to borrow when money is cheap.

The confusion between debt and deficit in everyday life is dangerous. Most of us, including governments, live a cash-flow life, as long as money coming in covers money going out we rest content. That is risky. Tempting though it might be to increase your mortgage to finance a holiday it is increasing the debt to cover a deficit. That is to short-change the future and it is dangerous, for governments as well as individuals. The UK government's decision to allow pensioners to have full control of their pension savings on retirement is to be welcomed in that it treats its citizens as responsible individuals but makes it even more important that those citizens are aware of the difference between investment and expenditure. At their stage in life it can be tempting to live for the present and spend what should be invested for the years ahead, in the hope that the state will come to the rescue if need be.

The reality is that any such rescue is bound to be niggardly. Recent surveys reveal that the average Briton would like to retire at 63, go to live in a bungalow near the sea, 11 miles from their nearest offspring, and live for a further 25 years. They estimate that they would need a pension of £23,457 per annum according to a survey by True Potential, a financial technology company, in 2014. The evidence to date suggests that this is optimistic. To achieve such a pension they would have to squirrel away £10,425 a year for 45 years. On average the survey showed they only contributed £2,671 last year, enough for just five years at their wished-for standard of living. They need to redo their sums if they want to enjoy those 25 years. The even more staggering fact is that one-third of the people working in Britain today have no private pension and have made no calculations at all about life after work, apparently believing that something will turn up. They will have to work until they drop or depend on the generosity of the other taxpayers to make up any shortfall after they have used up their state pension, a generosity that will not be unlimited. We have yet to take on board the astounding fact that within two generations we have added 15 years to our lives without, however, working any longer. Most of us will work for 40 years and live on for another 30 years. Soon we may be in so-called retirement for as long as we have been working. It is a staggering thought.

Most countries, like Britain, administer a Ponzi-type system, the aim being restricted to the relief of poverty in old age, not to fund the whole of life after work. That has been one of the great misunderstandings. The state pension was never intended to provide for a comfortable life for all, only to keep us out of absolute poverty. For the employees of large organisations it has, in the past, been better. Unlike the state pension, occupational pensions, funded by contributions from employer and employee and often inflation-indexed, did provide the guarantee of a comfortable living beyond employment. The financial future for many was taken care of. Occupational pensions, however, have proved to be too costly for most organisations and are gradually being phased out, to be replaced by defined contribution schemes in which what you get is related to what you, and your employer, put in, with an auto-enrolment that requires employers to enrol every worker automatically in a very minimal pension scheme, unless he or she opts out. The protective shield has been largely removed. Everyone is increasingly on their own, responsible for financing their own life beyond employment, apart from a very basic poverty-relieving pension from the state. In such a situation it would be unrealistic to assume that more income will come from somewhere when you come to need it. Ponzi stops working at the end of life. You have to find it yourself, in advance.

The problem for most householders is that they are already up to their eyeballs in debt and have nothing to spare to put into savings. If interest rates in Britain rose to 3 per cent in 2015 the average householder would have to spend half of all take-home pay on the mortgage. And that's not counting any other debts that might be piling up. The easy way out would be via inflation that would, over time, reduce the real value of the debt. But governments would then move to curb the inflation by raising the interest rate, which would put up the cost of the mortgage. You can't win. It's a catch-22 situation.

Governments have a similar problem. Of course countries do not die, although they can go bankrupt, as Greece, Ireland and Portugal effectively did. But as the number of new taxpayers falls while the pensioners keep living longer the Ponzi equation begins to falter. It goes badly wrong in countries like Germany and Italy where the birth rate has dramatically reduced. China and Japan face the same problem, only larger. Add in the growing health costs of those pensioners and the looming problem looks like a crash-landing waiting to happen.

Governments, unlike us, can go on borrowing more and more, until the day comes when nobody wants to buy their bonds, a day which for countries like the USA, Germany or Britain could be a long way off. But bigger debt means bigger interest payments and therefore less money to make up the Ponzi gap. Like more ordinary folk, they can't win in the long run.

A Ponzi mindset has come to be endemic in modern society. It is too easy to live in the present and let the future take care of itself. Except that it never does. Borrowing from the future to pay for today is made all too easy by those who make their money from our liabilities. Payday loans, logbook finance, where people borrow against their cars, interest-free offers from retailers, all encourage us to postpone the payback day and hope that something will turn up before it is too late. Ponzi thinking is addictive, and dangerous. We can lose control of our lives, living at the behest of our creditors. Governments cannot save us from ourselves, nor would we want them to. Indeed, in their eagerness to grow the economy and encourage consumption they are unlikely to try to curb our enthusiasm to borrow to spend. It is up to us alone. Governments could perhaps help, however.

One suggestion is that there should be a one-off cancellation of all household mortgages, what financiers would call a universal haircut for banks and insurance companies. There would be shrieks of outrage but the sudden release of money would trigger a spending spree and a rise in the economy that would help to compensate. The likelihood of any government enacting such a draconian policy must be minuscule, but a moderated version that, for example, required all mortgages to be extended in length by 50 per cent, might be possible.

Alternatively and more usefully, governments could help us to discipline ourselves by requiring all borrowers to provide details of their existing financial state when applying for a loan of any sort. This is already happening in Britain, with increasingly stringent requirements for affordability tests for mortgages and payday loans. That requirement in itself could be a wake-up call to review one's whole financial situation, including provision for the longer-term future. Credit and affordability checks in themselves are not enough. They do provide useful warning signs but they don't provide the answers to the problems they throw up, other than to say you can't have this loan or this purchase. That protects but does not teach. Both those checks need to be accompanied by more advice on financial management. Those who fail the checks might be offered free courses, rather as drivers in Britain with minor speeding offences are offered the choice of points on their driving licence or a one-day course on road safety. Do nothing and the danger is that we learn the lessons too late to do anything about them.

More fundamentally, most countries need a complete rethink of their approach to lifetime financial planning now that life goes on so much longer. One possible Second Curve would be to follow the example of Singapore, which imposes a degree of prudence on its citizens. Its Central Provident Fund collects 16 per cent of gross pay from the employer for each employee and 20 per cent from that same employee. This gets invested by the government and is available to the individual, with conditions, to pay for retirement and to help with housing, health care and insurance. It is the individual's own money, guarded for them, and it can be taken away with them if they leave permanently. Meantime it is a source of funds for the government. No trace of Ponzi there. Interestingly, it was introduced to Singapore by the British colonial administration in 1955 when Singapore was a small and fledgling state. As with the Beveridge plan it would take many years to be fully operational, but the current National Insurance and occupational schemes could be blended into a modified Singaporean fund. It would make it clearer to everyone what level of money they had stored up for the future, an essential for self-responsibility. As with every Second Curve outlined in this collection of essays it would require political courage to initiate, something that is rare in a democratic system, as I discuss in Essay 14.

The problem with the self-responsible society, the one that we are slowly becoming, is that we have to learn how to educate ourselves in areas that we did not need to worry about before, because someone else was taking care of them. Financial literacy, understanding how the money world works, is one of those areas and it does not come easy. The first lessons may start at school but, as I argue in Essay 13, what is learnt there is soon forgotten unless put to use right away. Fortunately perhaps, serious financial problems do not crop up for the young until long after the lessons of the classroom have faded away.

Carlo Ponzi, the dishwasher from Parma, turned Charles Ponzi, American temporary millionaire, has a lot to answer for. We also need to remember that he died a pauper.

11

THE JUST SOCIETY

What is fair?

JUSTICE IS ONE of those confusing words that can mean at least three very different things. It can mean giving people what they deserve, by way of either reward or punishment. Or it can mean giving people what they need. Or, again, it can mean fairness, which seeks to balance both the other meanings, defined by some as giving everyone the same unless it can be demonstrated that by giving some people more it will in some way be good for everyone. Not surprisingly these different understandings of what justice means can cause much confusion and a lot of conflict.

The rampant inequality, for instance, in modern society seems grossly unfair, but is it unjust? The gap between the 1 per cent and the 99 per cent increases each year. The 1 per cent argue that they deserve their rewards as the fruits of their enterprise and responsibilities. By their definition it is just. The rest complain that the benefits of a growing economy are not being shared with them; that their living standards are falling, with some in real poverty; and, in many cases, that their basic needs are not being met. This, they say, is unjust and unfair in what is supposed to be a democracy. Who is right? Everyone, depending on your point of view and your definition of justice.

The French economist Thomas Piketty has demonstrated, in his book *Capital in the 21st Century*, that when the rate of return on capital is greater than the growth rate of the economy as a whole, wealth inequality rises inexorably. Money makes money. In years gone by most wealth came from inheritance. The characters in the novels of Balzac and Jane Austen, Piketty points out, are endlessly concerned with the problems of inheritance: who will get it, how to keep it, who to pass it on to. Inheritance is where wealth came from in those days, as it has done throughout history. The 20th century, however, was different, and exceptional. The two world wars along with decolonisation eroded the capital base as capital was requisitioned, taxed or nationalised to pay for the wars and the subsequent welfare states. Meantime the economies of the West grew unusually fast due to the rebuilding of Europe and a technological catch-up. The economies grew faster than the return on capital and wealth was levelled out to some extent. In the 1980s, Piketty says, these processes went into reverse. Growth rates slowed, capital was rebuilt and taxes on high earnings were cut. When taxes were high there was little point in people awarding themselves high pay rises. Now that they could keep most of it, those at the top of corporations started rewarding themselves extravagantly. Today wealth holdings in the advanced economies are six times as large as the annual national income, the same level as before the First World War.

The difference is that the new wealth is owned and earned, not by the landowners of old, but by the 'working rich', mainly the top executives of corporate firms, along with a few bankers and the occasional sports star, who together make up just .01 per cent of the population. Piketty calls this situation 'meritocratic extremism'. That is a polite term for excessive greed. I have never seen the sense of the bonus culture. To me it seems demeaning to have to be bribed to do your best in your job. When I worked in one of the corporate elephants it was assumed that your salary was the appropriate rate for your work and you were expected to do it to the best of your ability. Success was eventually rewarded by promotion and, with it, an increased salary. It becomes absurd when some bonuses are guaranteed or, if not guaranteed, have become so much the norm that they are part of the implied contract. There is, after all, no evidence that the possibility of a higher bonus produces more or better work.

This is compounded by the remuneration committees of the corporate world. These allow the senior executives to disclaim any responsibility for their excessive rewards. 'Nothing to do with me,' they say, 'these things are decided independently by the remuneration committee.'

Most remuneration committees, however, seek to establish the norm for the industry and, as long as the performance justifies it, to pay a little above the average. To do less would indicate that they judged the performance unsatisfactory, which they would only do in extreme circumstances. The result is, inevitably, a constantly rising average, unrelated to any world beyond the one they know. It is the perfect self-validating system, impervious to outside influence. Should outsiders be included? You might think so but that would require a change to the rules of corporate governance which, of course, are set by the board itself.

We do not grudge successful sports stars or entrepreneurs their earnings, which we attribute to their special skills. The irony is that neither the sports hero nor the entrepreneur does it for the money. They do it because they love it and are good at it. The money is nice but not the point. It is when money becomes the point that something goes wrong. As I have argued in Essay 7 it was the new, and mistaken, priority given to shareholder value in the 1970s that made money the main point of business, leading to the share options and bonuses which distorted the priorities of the managers, and to the harmful emphasis on the short term. The replacement of the bonus culture by profit-sharing, and share-option schemes by wider share ownership, would turn things around. Money would be the prize but not the point. There is a difference. Ask any prize-winner, be they Nobel or gold medallist.

Nevertheless, as it is, the recipients of the high pay awards see these as the fruits of enterprise, well deserved and just. Without such high compensation they would not be able to accumulate capital, which, they feel, would be unfair. On the contrary, say the other 99 per cent, it is the high compensation that is unfair because it is so disproportionate. After all, much of the success of those at the top is due to the work of those below. A lot of other people work hard but are not rewarded in the same way, even though many of them – doctors, teachers, nurses and others – contribute hugely to society. The three faces of justice are in conflict and the prognosis is not good.

In the coming generation we may see the worst of two past worlds, a group of people living off the wealth built up by the previous generation and a continuation of the extreme pay to top people, as the return on capital continues to exceed the rate of growth in the economies. The new *rentiers*, those who will be living off inherited capital, are unlikely to have inherited the social responsibility that often accompanied such riches in past centuries. I argued in Essay 7 that capitalism and democracy are uneasy bedfellows, that if the former is to survive it must be seen to benefit all not just a favoured few. This is perhaps the most urgent problem facing us today, to restore a proper justice to the creation and distribution of wealth. Wealth has to be spread around more widely without destroying the motivation to create it in the first place.

We could always call their bluff, the bluff of those who assert that high rewards are needed to retain their talent. Many would be happy to work for less if that became the norm. If they didn't, there must be others equally talented who would. The pool of potential senior executives is neither as small nor as exclusive as those inside it consider it to be. The problem is to create the norm. The European Commission has tried to limit bonuses to some multiple of the annual salary. In response the organisations just bump up the salaries. Many of the Swiss wanted to restrict top pay to 12 times the pay of the lowest-paid worker. It narrowly failed in the following referendum. Maybe if the multiple had been 30 it would have passed, although in many large American businesses the multiple is now over 400. Plato suggested four as the ideal but organisations were much smaller then. I once sat on the board of a company owned by the workforce where the multiple was seven. To increase the pay of the chief executive, all that was needed was to raise the pay of those at the bottom. That worked for everyone until they realised that they could outsource the cheaper work, thereby creating a new and higher base level and higher salaries at the top. It was just bad luck for those who had to leave.

There are always ways round these things but ideally such a formula, adjusted for the size of the organisation and even for the type of industry, would encourage productivity which would, in turn, allow an organisation to pay more to those at the bottom without harming its profitability. If that were accompanied by a profit-sharing scheme related to base salary it would allow a proportional level of reward for everyone, including the senior executives. If that formula were to be internationally agreed that would be even better. Even if it weren't an international norm there is no evidence that there would be a mass migration of talent in search of more exotic rewards. Money, I sometimes think, is often rightly called compensation, compensation for stressful, tedious or pointless work in unpleasing surroundings. Not everyone would judge the extra compensation to be enough for the pain and upheaval of moving home and family to the other side of the world. Brave organisations could try it and see. So could governments.

What are the alternatives? Punitive taxation on the wealth or income of the top earners is counterproductive. Make the taxation too high and those high earners will leave or find ways around it. Nor will competition solve the problem; it might even make it worse in a winner-takes-all world, making the successful even richer. We need, instead, to start at the beginning, where the wealth is created, to look to the institutions, to the way they are designed and governed, to citizen companies and profit-sharing rather than arbitrary bonuses, to better corporate governance, to improved education and, perhaps, to trade unions reinvented as professional organisations, the last especially. We miss the countervailing power of the trade unions, who have stuck to their old power bases in the large organisations, now mainly confined to the public sector, and seem to ignore the opportunities open to them as the champions of the self-employed and the proprietors of small businesses, the new and growing workforce.

Pre-distribution, the economists call it – making the system fairer to begin with, rather than compensating for its deficiencies after the fact – an ugly word for an important point. If the trade unions can't or won't do it, maybe governments should. Twenty years ago I met with a group of trade-union leaders at Ruskin College to share with them my view of how the workforce would be changing with, I suggested, a rapidly growing sector of self-employment and a part-time fringe. Here, I said, is the new opportunity for the union movement, because these people will need all the help that they can get. They shook their heads. No, they said, our future lies with the big organisations. Ask now how it is that a cleaner in New York earns three times as much as one in London, despite a lower minimum wage, and the answer is plain: it is union power ensuring a bit of that pre-distribution.

What then, in default of union action, could governments do? Why not, for a start, significantly raise the national minimum wage that is now a feature of most of the advanced economies? Raise it enough to create a proper living wage, adjusted to fit the cost of living in different parts of the country. The increase should be high enough to force businesses to raise their productivity to pay for it, which would, in the short term, mean cutting some jobs. That could be a price worth paying to get the economies back on track. At present productivity levels in Britain are far too low, mainly because labour is cheap so that more are employed than are strictly needed, which in turn keeps wages low. Labour is cheap partly because there are too many people prepared to work for too little but also because the UK government subsidises the wages of low-paid workers with in-work benefits. To me it makes no sense. Why should the taxpayer subsidise the employers, allowing them to get by with cheap labour instead of raising their productivity so that they can afford to pay proper wages? Those in-work benefits in Britain cost £28 billion in 2013. That is a big subsidy and, I would argue, counterproductive in the long run. Pre-distribution, or starting at the beginning, should mean paying good money for good work. As it is, with such an abundance of cheap subsidised labour on offer, there is no incentive to invest in new equipment or in training to improve productivity. Make labour expensive and employers will have to respond.

It would be a Second Curve that might be nasty but nice in the end. It would be nasty because it would put many out of work. Nevertheless it would cost less overall to support those out of work in community work, training and education than keeping many more of them in subsidised and unproductive jobs. Some argue for a 'basic income' scheme, an income given to all citizens above and between certain ages, enough for a basic standard of living, but not big enough to deter anyone from taking on paid work. The Swiss will shortly have a referendum on such a scheme set at 30,000 Swiss francs (around £20,000). Such schemes, although superficially attractive, have always proved economically unrealistic. The proposed reform to the British benefit system, if it works, will be, in effect, a guarantee of income support to the worst off, a partial basic income.

A further distortion of the just society, particularly in London, is the price of housing. An average house price of £500,000 effectively excludes most young couples from the property market and creates severe problems for the service sector, including the health and education services, when their essential staff have nowhere local to live. The hope is that an increasing supply of housing will eventually bring prices down, but 'eventually' is shorthand for a very distant future. Meantime a Second Curve would seek to make two changes. In the first place governments might start to alter the tax-free status of the sale of the main home.

I was speaking to a young woman who had, a few years ago, given up her job as a journalist to care for her young family. Now that the family were all in school was she, I asked, going back to her journalist career? 'Oh no,' she said, 'I'm in the moving house business now. It's hard work but much more profitable.' 'What do you mean?' I asked. 'Well,' she replied, 'last year we sold our house in quite a fashionable area, moved half a mile further out to a larger house and made £400,000 net profit. I guess we might do it again in a few years.'

Something is wrong if you can make more money while you sleep than if you go out to work. That £400,000 should be taxed. Of course, like many of my suggested Second Curves, it would be politically difficult, so it would need to be graduated and only applied to houses above the national or local average house price, so that the lower-paid are not unduly penalised. The result, however, would be a fall in house prices and an end to my journalist friend's continual home moves. It would reduce mobility but it would not be unfair; people would only be paying tax on extra money, which by definition they would have the means to pay.

It might also make people ponder the wisdom of the pressing desire, in Britain especially, to own one's own home as soon as one can. It does not make economic sense that the savings of a nation should go disproportionately into property, which produces no useful wealth for the country and very few jobs, and which, in turn, makes it more profitable for the banks to follow suit with their loans, thereby starving business of much-needed finance for growth. I grew up in a tied house – my father was a pastor – and I then lived in rented accommodation until I was 50, by which time I knew more or less for sure where I wanted to spend the rest of my life, and this, indeed, is where we have lived ever since. Theoretically, it makes sense to rent for the first half of your life; it gives you flexibility and less responsibility: if the boiler bursts ring the landlord and go to sleep. But renting only works if there is a stable property market, which would happen if the sales tax were to be imposed. Several birds would be killed by this one stone: property prices would come down, more people would rent, making it easier to move to where the work was, and less money would go into property, freeing up bank finance for more useful investment. It would be a difficult reform but essential if our savings are not to be eaten up by mortgages and, as a result, our businesses starved of customers with money left in their pockets.

I wonder, however, if, in our agonising over the rampant inequality at the top of society, we might be missing the more important issue. Yes, it seems unfair that some few, by a mixture of luck, clever accountants and good judgement, are much richer than the rest of us, but the truth probably is that such people live in a very different world, one which, even in our dreams, most of us would not want to inhabit. Nor would it help to spread their wealth around, or cap it in some way. The richest 50 people in the world may have an aggregate wealth equal to that of the poorest half of the world's population, but sharing it out over that half would be just pennies in each person's pocket. In short, it would make no difference to most of our lives if the top 1 per cent were poorer, so, unfair though we might think it, perhaps we should ignore the 1 per cent and concentrate on what is the real injustice, not of wealth but of work, or the lack of it.

The real inequality and unfairness in modern capitalism is going to be the lack of meaningful work for the less skilled and less talented among us, and there are many millions of them. As I have argued in other essays, robots of one sort or another will deal with much of the routine work. A lot more will be outsourced to cheaper sources of labour abroad. There will be much less for the less skilled worker to do. I used to give hairdressing as an example of work that could not be sent abroad or replaced by a computer, until an executive from Google told me that a machine was in development that would shape your hair to your design when placed over your head. Not to everyone's taste perhaps, but one more example of a cheaper do-it-yourself way. Factories, coal mines and steelworks used to be the work providers, but most of these have long gone. There is little left of manufacturing except the high-end jobs in design and marketing, the rest have been exported and won't return.

We are left with the people-caring jobs in hospitals, social work, schools, prisons, law courts and local government. The trouble is that these are, by definition, jobs that can only be done by people, and people with the personal skills to do them are increasingly expensive. We want as few of them as possible to keep the cost down. It is a catch-22 situation. We need more people-heavy jobs but we can't afford more people. Nor are the jobs

on offer necessarily the sort that will appeal to those of
the young who look for more physically challenging
work. Not everything is bleak, however. At the beginning of the last century the largest category of employment was domestic service. As I pointed out in Essay
4, 'The Workplace', it is so once again, but this time
with a difference. Most of the new domestic workers
are self-employed. One consequence of the new rich has
been an increase in these domestic services – childcare,
cleaning, chauffeuring, gardening, dog-walking, shopping, cooking and secretarial, to name but a few of the
services that the rich now want. It is no accident that
the majority of the new jobs created in Britain in recent
years have been in these flea-type microbusinesses.
Perhaps we need the plutocrats after all to give them
the work.

Even so, there will still be too little for many of
the less educated to do. That is the real injustice,
undeserved and unprepared for. To remedy it we need
a massive injection of funds to provide better education
and training, including the encouragement of self-
employment and apprenticeships. As I argue in Essay
13, 'The Schools of the Future', that requires an education which develops social as well as intellectual skills,
much of that education happening at work. We should
also look backwards for once. Our ancestors learnt how
to work at work, earning while they learnt. We need to
do more of that, multiplying the apprenticeships many
times over and encouraging employers to see it as part

of their social responsibility. That all costs money. Rather than pay for it out of general taxation perhaps a special fund should be created, possibly paid for by the tax on the sale of one's home, which could be used to allow all work-based education to be tax-deductible and to pay a subsistence wage to the learners.

We have, for centuries, grown up in an employment system that is top-down. Work for most has been created for us by institutions, both in the public and private sectors. We have forgotten that those institutions were once created out of nothing. They are now paring down so the system needs to be restarted from the bottom again, through small-scale entrepreneurial ventures that, if successful, build up and create work for others. It happened before, when the new technologies of what came to be called the Industrial Revolution saw thousands of new flowers of business blossom and flourish. It can happen again, but we have to prepare the seedbeds for the new flowers and help them through their early days. Schools, colleges, banks and venture capitalists, businesses and government agencies need to combine to pump-start a new enterprise-led revolution. In the long term only that sort of Second Curve will remedy the injustices built up during the last phases of the current one.

12

THE GOLDEN SEEDS

Do you know your own capability?

FOR ONE OF my big birthdays our two children gave me a small sculpture that they had commissioned. It was in the shape and colour of two intertwined golden tears. Odd, I thought: what was there to cry about on such a happy occasion? They were not tears, they hastily explained, but golden seeds. They knew that one of my favourite concepts was that of the golden seed. It is part of my optimistic belief in humanity that there exists in each of us the seed of possibility. This is our 'golden seed' which, if we only knew what it was, and if it were to be fertilised, watered and cared for, might lead to personal fulfilment. The best gift that you can give anyone, I maintain, is to help them to find and grow their golden seed.

Marianne Williamson puts it more poetically in her book *A Return to Love*: 'We ask ourselves, "Who am I to be brilliant, gorgeous, talented and fabulous?" Actually who are you not to be? You are a child of God . . . We were born to make manifest the glory of

God that is within us. It's not just in some of us; it's in everyone.' More prosaically, Martha Nussbaum and Amartya Sen, two distinguished academics, have written about our 'capabilities', which are, says Nussbaum, 'not just abilities residing inside a person but also the freedoms or opportunities created by a combination of personal abilities and the political, social and economic environment'. She is making the point that society as a whole has a responsibility to allow our seeds to grow.

In a study that my wife and I did of entrepreneurs in business, the arts and the community, *The New Alchemists*, we found that it was the discovery of that golden seed in each of them that gave them a nugget of self-belief, which in turn gave them the confidence to pursue their ideas. Sometimes you stumble across it. In our study Philip Hughes was a frustrated sales engineer for an oil company when he bought a book on computing, a new topic in the early sixties, and 'like a flash of light I knew instantly what I wanted to do'. His aptitude for this new technology was to prove his golden seed. Passing by a shop window, which was the front window of something called a software consulting company, he went in, got a job and went on to found Logica, one of Britain's earliest and biggest computer consulting firms. His story is interesting because his other lurking golden seed was his talent as an artist and he later had a distinguished artistic career, including the Chairmanship of the Trustees of the National Gallery in London.

Sometimes you know it from the beginning. Terence Conran was making dolls' houses at the age of 12 and selling them in local shops. He went on to found Habitat and changed the way British people furnished their homes. Food was always his other passion and, again, he turned it into a successful business empire, starting with what he called a restaurant without chefs, a soup kitchen in London filled with his own furniture. At other times, someone spots the seed in you. William Atkinson, one of Britain's great head teachers, had the good fortune to catch the attention of one of his own teachers, who spotted his potential some years after his arrival in England from Jamaica and encouraged him to be a teacher and to believe in himself.

These are three unusual people, but aren't we all unusual in our own ways? Why do we often want to be like everyone else? Each one of us has something special about us, if only we could unearth it from the daily trudge of our lives and then do something to bring that seed to life. In 1983 Howard Gardner of Harvard University revolutionised much of our thinking on intelligence with his theory of multiple intelligences. He demonstrated that there is not one form of intellectual competence, such as IQ, but several different types that are not necessarily related. This realisation is not new. The Greek poet Archilochus divided the world into hedgehogs who saw all intelligence as one piece, with some having more of it than others, and foxes who believed that there were many different aspects of it. Later, in the 18th century Franz Joseph Gall, a physicist who specialised in phrenology, the study of the shape and size of the brain, nominated 37 different human faculties or powers. What Gardner did was to specify the principal ones as he saw them and to spell out some of their characteristics and the implications for education.

We do not have to immerse ourselves in the details of Gardner's thesis or even to agree with his list of intelligences to realise how well his ideas march with our intuitive perceptions of individual differences. Gardner himself identified seven types of intelligence:

> Linguistic intelligence
> Logical-mathematical intelligence
> Musical intelligence
> Spatial intelligence
> Bodily-kinaesthetic intelligence
> Intrapersonal intelligence
> Interpersonal intelligence

Importantly, the different intelligences are not connected. You can be a talented athlete (bodily-kinaesthetic) but no good in class when studying logical-mathematical topics. Popular musicians have often left school feeling a failure, only to go on to make fortunes. That said, Gardner suggests that success often requires two or more of the intelligences to be combined. Gardner was concerned to redefine traditional views of intelligence, but the word itself is unnecessarily limiting in common usage. Talent, aptitude, skill or competence are all versions of intelligence. Gardner and his colleagues later identified 20 varieties of what they called intelligence.

The problem is that formal education systems focus on the first two, linguistic and logical-mathematical, and largely ignore the others, although the two personal intelligences are the ones most crucial to life and work. Intrapersonal intelligence is all about understanding oneself and interpersonal intelligence is to do with understanding others. Both are central to successful relationships at home and at work and were later to be combined and extended by Daniel Goleman as emotional intelligence. To Gardner's list I would add creative intelligence, which Gardner would include under spatial intelligence, referencing artists in particular, but which, from our experience of our Alchemists, should also include imagination, the capacity to see the world differently through what Jeff Grout and Liz Fisher called the 'third eye' in their own study of entrepreneurs.

The majority of the Alchemists whom we studied found that the schools that they attended were too restrictive. They left or, if they stayed, did not perform well. Their own set of intellectual competences did not fit the standard curriculum, which emphasises the first two types of intelligence and pays too little attention to the other five. Gardner would not have been surprised. In conversation with Goleman he said, '. . . we subject everyone to an education where, if you succeed, you will be best suited to be a college professor. And we evaluate everyone along the way according to whether they meet that narrow standard of success. We should spend less time ranking children and more time helping them to identify their natural competencies and gifts, and cultivate those. There are hundreds and hundreds of way to succeed, and many, many different abilities that will help you get there.'

I once spoke with a professor of English at Cambridge University. The English course at Cambridge is very popular and can take its pick from a talented group of applicants, most of whom do not go on to make any direct use of their degree, as in teaching or research. Instead, many of them rise to occupy important roles in society. 'In view of that,' I asked the professor, 'what advice or help do you give them to prepare for their future responsibilities?' 'That's none of my business,' he replied. 'They come here to read English and read English is what they do. Everything else they will have to pick up on the streets.' He was within his rights, but his limited view of the role of education ripples down the levels to the feeder schools who find themselves forced to take a similarly narrow view of their role and responsibilities if they are to secure a place for their students at any prestigious university. So it is that many other competences can escape notice, often until it is too late to revive the seed. It could be argued that universities are largely responsible for the flaws in our school systems because we have allowed their preoccupation with academic and intellectual studies to shape the curriculum and priorities of the schools.

Cutting this link will require us to rethink the role of the university, to recognise that the traditional academic degree is not for everyone, that the democratisation of university education is too expensive and unhelpful to many, that a modular approach that allowed for more competence-based courses would be both cheaper and more suited to a world where the demands and shape of work are changing so rapidly. If the link with schools were then to be weakened it might allow the schools to get back to what they were intended for, preparing the young for life in its broadest sense, recognising that everyone is both different and special. Ideally we should aim for an individual curriculum, one tailored to the needs of each child, rather than a national curriculum that seeks to make every child the same. To the outsider it often seems that schools are designed to suit the teachers and the system rather than the students, an inversion of good organisational practice. But if we cannot treat children as unique individuals in school, because it might be too managerially inconvenient, then we can make up for it later. Golden seeds do not disappear – they just lie hidden, awaiting discovery.

We can all make our own list of the different

competences, skills and talents, intellectual or otherwise, that we can see in ourselves. The point is that
any one of them can be the seed of our future if we
cultivate it, and are helped to do so. Some have that
light-bulb moment when they glimpse their possibility
and the seed of their future life. Most of us will need
help to spot the seed, conditioned as we are to judge
ourselves by the criteria set by the prevailing culture.
The early seed spotting should be the first concern of
the parents. It is tempting at first to want your offspring
to conform to the pathways and stages of development
followed by other children of the same age. But that
may get in the way of the seed-spotting process.
Capability Brown, the great landscape architect of
18th-century Britain, got his nickname because when
viewing an estate that might be a project for him, he
would often tell his clients that 'it has great capabilities', meaning potential.

Capability is there in all children if we could learn
to look at them with that third eye, to see differences
as clues, not necessarily as faults to be corrected.
Nonconformists may be a nuisance but may actually
be artists in the process of development. In our study
of the Alchemists it was noteworthy that most of them
were second or third children, often less strictly disciplined, with less expected of them initially, more free
therefore to be different. In a presidential address that
I once gave to the North of England Education
Conference I made this point and argued that a little

naughtiness in school should be tolerated as long as it did no harm to the other children. It could, I argued, be a sign of the stirring of creativity or at least a desire to express one's individuality. The classroom should be designed for the students, not for the convenience of the teacher. My speech was roundly condemned by the teacher unions who could imagine only chaos in their classrooms, which rather proved my point, I thought. My own view was that the traditional classrooms were inimical to learning and needed to be rethought and redesigned in the light of the new technologies. Formal education is, however, only one part of our early development. The truth is that the nurturing of the golden seed is best done by a mentor. That mentor can be sought out or appointed but more often happens by fortuitous chance, when someone spots potential in someone in their charge or in their orbit, takes an interest, the chemistry works and both parties profit, because the pleasure in fostering the growth of another is very real.

Teachers would like to think that they act as seed nurturers to all the young people in their care, but that has to be wishful thinking, given the constraints of the system. Luckily there are many other seed nurturers, starting with parents who can often have too narrow a view of what constitutes success. It can be disconcerting to see your child develop interests and aptitudes so very different from your own. When our son declared that he would be turning down his university place to realise his ambition to be the lead singer in a band, it took a lot of self-containment to tell him that I recognised his ambition and to encourage him to go ahead. Fortunately, or perhaps not, he changed his mind. Perhaps he was only testing my tolerance of his independence, but he made me aware that while most parents would like to think that they are good nurturers of likely seeds they are not always the best seed spotters.

When they were redecorating one of the very first and oldest classrooms at Eton they discovered underneath the plaster a painting on the original 15th-century wall. Under the painting was a Latin motto, *Virtus preceptoris est ingeniorum notare discrimina*, which, roughly translated, reads: 'The virtue of a teacher is to heed the differences of [boys'] abilities.' Six hundred years ago good teachers were spotting golden seeds.

For many young people it is during their late teenage years, a time when they are forging their identities, that they need most help in unearthing their unique golden seed. For some of our Alchemists it was their first boss, for one the local priest, for others a teacher past or present. We all need mentors. Lucky are those who find them at that stage. For some, however, the seeds lie dormant for the first half of their life. One study that my wife and I did was entitled *Reinvented Lives: Women at Sixty*. In this book we interviewed 28 women who, in their sixties, reinvented themselves to live a new life, often realising an ambition that had been delayed while they brought up a family, but often discovering talents in themselves that they had not realised that they had. It is never too late. One of them became ordained as a priest, another fulfilled a long ambition to work at the South Pole after a life of writing children's books and raising her family. A third wanted to help out her daughter and found herself running a café in a seaside town and being rather good at it. It is never too late to dig up your seed and start a new curve in life.

The new curve of work, with formal careers for many finishing earlier and many more people turning to self-employment of one sort or another, is an opportunity to do a bit of seed spotting in oneself, for seeds often lie dormant for years, only to spring to life when triggered by accident or necessity. When I was about to leave for my first overseas posting with my oil company my mother, who was, I knew, not at all pleased by my choice of career, came to see me off. 'Never mind, dear,' were her parting words, 'it will all be good material for your book.' I looked at her, puzzled, as the car pulled away. What on earth was she talking about? I was not going to write any books, I was about to be an oil executive with little time to read books, let alone write them. Twenty years later, no longer an oilman, I was sitting in a Provençal farmhouse with my family, writing my first book and relishing the experience. I am still doing it. My mother had spotted a seed even though it took a while to germinate.

I hadn't worked out my ideas on lurking golden

seeds back then so I don't think I ever told her how right she had been, both about the books, and about the material for them. Her unsolicited advice continued, although not intended as such. I had presented her with a copy of that first book, one that was, in retrospect, a bit academically pretentious, a textbook on management. I noticed that she had not got beyond page ten. 'Don't you like it?' I asked. 'I don't know why you need to use all those new words,' she replied. 'Surely there are enough in the Book of Common Prayer and the works of Shakespeare to cover all you need to say.' It was the best editorial advice I have ever been given. Seeds need shaping, sometimes even pruning once they start to grow, and, yes, occasionally parents – especially mothers – can spot seeds.

Today the world is full of sprouting seeds. The internet is a greenhouse full of seedbeds for new businesses. It has lowered the cost of entry, particularly for service enterprises. It is an exciting time. Not all the seeds will turn out to be golden; some will fail to germinate at all. It does not matter. The very fact that you have created something unique is proof of Marianne Williamson's poetic assertion that each one of us is special. My wife, a portrait photographer, and I are documenting, in words and photographs, the projects of young entrepreneurs in less affluent parts of London to give hope and encouragement to others to follow their example. It is heart-warming to see the pride in the faces of these young men and women as they stand to be photographed. They carry with them the tools of their trade and their business cards, the evidence of their sprouting seeds. It may not turn out to be their golden one, but that does not matter, they tell us. They already have something to be proud of, and there will be other seeds and new curves to come. Of that they are sure.

13

THE SCHOOLS OF THE FUTURE

What might education look like?

I HAD WHAT was seen at the time to be a good education, good enough to get a full scholarship to my secondary independent school in Britain and then a scholarship to Oxford University. Looking back, however, I don't remember much of it, probably because I never used most of it again. But I did leave with one lesson that deeply influenced my later life, although it was a lesson that no one intended. I learnt that in the world ahead of me all problems had already been solved. The answers, I gathered, were known to my teachers, or were in the back of their textbooks. My job was to commit those answers to memory and reproduce them on demand, initially in examinations and thereafter, I assumed, in my life.

To put it another way, the problems that I studied at school were all closed problems with proven answers. How far is it to Birmingham by road is a closed problem. Why should we go to Birmingham is an open one, with any number of possible answers, depending on the context. My school education was actually harmful since most of the problems that I was to face in work and life were open problems: Should I marry this woman? Buy this house? Trust this person? Take this job? Invest in this business? Obey this command? Even simple things like choosing a restaurant or buying clothes turned out to be open questions. At first I assumed that there were right answers to these questions, the difficulty being that I didn't know them. The right thing to do, then, was to find someone or some book that might give me answers or tell me what to do. I was soon categorised as an indecisive conformist, a person with few opinions of his own. Dull, boring and, I was repeatedly told by my bosses, lacking in initiative. You could say that my school might have ruined my life, even while proclaiming me as one of their most successful students.

Fortunately, the last half of my degree course at Oxford was devoted to history and philosophy, two subjects that can be approached in two very different ways. You can 'learn' history by studying and memorising the key facts, and philosophy by ploughing through the theories of leading philosophers. That was not the approach offered to me.

'I want a 3,000-word essay on Truth, by next week,' my philosophy tutor said to me. 'You may want to see what some other thinkers made of it, but I am only interested in what you think and why.' I went away thinking that this would be easy, for surely we all know the difference between truth and falsehood. Four sleepless nights later I knew differently. I had to think for myself, using other sources for inspiration but not for certainty. The same with history. 'What combination of personalities and factors was responsible for the outbreak of that war?' would be a typical assignment. On one occasion, hard pressed for time, I copied out a passage from a distinguished historian. When I reached that point, reading my essay out aloud as we were required to do, my tutor said nothing, but walked over to his bookcase, took down the works of said historian, rummaged through the pages until he reached the crucial point, then just went on reading aloud the sentences following my bit. Nothing more was said. I got the point. He was interested in my thoughts, not those of other experts.

Eventually I realised that I was not being taught philosophy or history but more fundamentally how to think and how to learn. That is very different from adding to what you know. I had a friend once who was a walking encyclopedia; he knew everything, except how to use most of it. One of his friends once said of him, 'He is very intelligent but he can't run a bath, let alone a department.' My final university examination papers had twenty questions, of which I only had to answer four. I left with a top degree without knowing the whole syllabus or even most of it. I felt a bit of a cheat until I realised that the examiners were not interested in how much I knew but in how well I had learnt to deal with each situation that I was presented with, using relevant facts where appropriate. Knowledge evaporates, learnt skills live on. You never forget how to ride a bicycle.

True learning, I was later to understand, starts with curiosity, with a problem or a challenge, a question that you need to answer. That is followed by a search for ideas and information which in turn allow you to form a hypothesis or possible solution. This solution then needs to be tested and the outcome reflected upon, which will often lead to a further question. This 'circle of learning' is done intuitively by children or more consciously now by me for these essays. Ever since university I have been more interested in the *process* of education then the *content*, believing that content can always be found when needed but the process has to be learnt young. When later I applied for a job in the oil industry I apologised to the selection committee that I knew nothing of oil or of business. They said, 'Don't worry. You have a well-trained mind which we can fill with all the content you need.' That was reassuring, but as I was to discover it is not enough to be able to learn and to think, you must also work out how to do and to be. As I have since come to realise, learning never stops, it lasts until you die.

I am now sure of the following:

That learning to think or to do is as important as learning facts.

That learning is mostly experience understood on
   reflection.
That teachers usually learn more than their pupils.
That the curiosity or the need to learn is crucial.
That learning that is unused soon disappears.
That no one is stupid, just not interested or curious.

I know some other things from my later work experience:

That three or four heads are better than one in
   most situations.
That not all learning, or even most, happens in a
   classroom.
That mixed ability should mean a mix of
   different abilities, not different levels of the
   same abilities.
That we all have a bit of the teacher in us.

That last point matters. Wikipedia would not exist were
it not for the thousands of individuals who want to
contribute what they know to the site. YouTube is awash
with helpful hints and instructions on how to fix
anything from your vacuum cleaner to your marriage,
many of which are uploaded anonymously and for no
reward. We love contributing our special expertise. We
love to teach and that, I believe, is how we learn best.
It follows that turning students into teachers of others
is the best way for them to learn. Instead of the teacher
instructing the class, get the students to do it. I tried

it with my own business students and it worked brilliantly. They learnt more, remembered more, enjoyed it more. I read the other day of a primary school teacher who asked her class of 9-year-olds to research the topic of electromagnetism on their iPads in their groups and then be prepared, after 40 minutes, to make a presentation to the class on what it is and why it matters to us today. I'm quite sure that they learnt more that way, and remembered more, than if they had listened to a lecture by her, brilliant though it might have been. High Tech High, a group of charter schools in San Diego, carries this principle to extremes, organising most of the learning around team-based creative projects, done outside the classroom as much as in it.

There are other ways too. Thirty years ago the Royal Society of Arts in London launched a campaign called Education for Capability, which I chaired for some years. Its purpose was to persuade schools and colleges to put some of these ideas into practice. Our view of education was based on seven 'C's – Cultivation, Comprehension, Creativity, Cooperation, Communication, Confidence and Competence. These seven elements were, in our estimation, essential for a full life in modern society. Cultivation and comprehension referred to the essential things and skills needed to play a part in society – the subjects conventionally taught in schools, principally English, history, mathematics and science and, now, technology including coding. In our view, these were essential skills and pieces of knowledge, but not enough by themselves, although even these need not be taught in traditional ways. The rest of the Cs were capacities that could be learnt but not taught, abilities essential to enable one to fulfil one's full potential or capability. By competence, I should explain, we meant any particular skill that gets things done. These capacities were best delivered, we believed, through practical projects or problems that had discernible outcomes. The campaign gave out awards to programmes and projects that lived up to our criteria. Many of them were outside the classroom, involving the arts, sports or entrepreneurial ventures. I have in the past suggested that these activities could be the responsibility of an alternative faculty, possibly including volunteers from the local community.

Education is meant to be a preparation for life. Its results therefore should properly be tested by the outcomes in life after education, but the time lapse is so long that it never gets done, except by anecdote at alumni gatherings. Examinations test only the absorption of knowledge shortly after its reception, not its use in life. It can lead to too much concentration on preparing students just for the examination. That's what crammers do, not educationalists. Why is Britain one of the few countries (if not the only one) that have a compulsory nationwide examination at 16? Why not have only a common school-leaving examination at 18, as in most other countries, leaving the school to use any intermediate tests that it considers useful? Better still, allow each school to set its own leaving examination, as in some states in America. We should trust our teachers more. As it is, education has come to resemble a game of croquet with a set of hoops to be negotiated along with complicated rules to make it more difficult. Croquet is my favourite sport but I am not surprised that so many of our guests refuse to play. They find it too frustrating and unrewarding. So too is education for many of our young people. We need to get rid of the hoops.

Artists of every sort learn by practice with help. We are all artists in that we are the creators of our own lives. We learn most about life from living, by practice with help. Impressed by the working knowledge of the young helpers in my local Apple store I asked about their training programme. 'There isn't one,' they said. 'We have to learn by eavesdropping on our savvier colleagues, by playing around on the machines when we have any free time, or by asking when we get stuck.' Just as my small grandchildren do, I thought.

The front-loading theory of education assumes that young people are prepared to take on board the proposition that what they are asked to learn will be useful one day and that it can all be safely warehoused until they need it. Deferred gratification of this sort is a tough ask of young people and, unsurprisingly, not usually successful. Learning without context is hard, and learning without use soon evaporates, as we discover when learning a new language. So much of what we spend our time on in schools must surely be wasted.

Instead, if we do learn most from living, we would do well to remember that the living starts early. The Jesuits are right to emphasise that the first seven years set the pattern for life.

The family has to be our first school. That is where curiosity is at its height, where unforced learning happens daily. 'Where did you learn how to work that iPad so well?' I asked my 6-year-old grandson. 'Dunno,' he said, 'I just did it and it worked.' He also speaks Greek and English quite unselfconsciously, having picked both up from his parents without any deliberate learning. It is in the family that character is formed. It is there that the young person learns, or should learn, how to cooperate, take responsibility, exercise self-control and be aware of the needs of others. Creativity is inborn in the very young, just bursting for opportunity, as is the desire to communicate. In other words, the components of Education for Capability are all there in the family, waiting to be developed, by example as much as by design. Unfortunately we cannot assume that all families will be good exemplars. Schools are too often left to make good the deficiencies. The first stage of a Second Curve in education, therefore, should be to find a way to help parents live up to their responsibilities as the heads of the first school for life.

In years gone by one moved from the family straight into work. Formal schooling has only been around for the last 200 years. You learnt about work at work. You still do. I did. If school is now a required interval between family and the real workplace then the school needs to offer an imitation of work and life beyond its boundaries. Unfortunately the image of a workplace that the young person carries away from their school is too often that of a factory, a hierarchical organisation with rigid rules demanding conformity, where the work is broken down into its component parts or piecework, where cooperation is viewed as collusion except in clearly demarcated exercises, where creativity is a nuisance and innovation is reserved for the hierarchy. To be effective as schools for life, the schools need to be more like work as it is today (or should be), where tasks are increasingly project-based, done in groups, where initiative is prized and commitment rewarded. You see this on the sports field and in drama and music productions where different skills and different ages combine to produce a performance of which they and their public can be proud. Why can this not be the norm in the rest of the school? As it is, the arts and sports are too often relegated to the periphery or left to the parents to provide. This cannot be right.

In one school that we visited as part of the Education for Capability campaign we were shown a project being done by a class that they had classified as remedial, for the slower learners. The class had been asked during that term to prepare and make a short three-minute television programme on road safety. On the day that we visited they were going to do the final shoot, having done the research, written the script and made some supporting illustrations. The young director (he was 14) was lining up the presenter who had to read from a primitive autocue written on cards. I was told that the group had deliberately picked the shyest boy among them to do the presentation because they hoped it would boost his self-confidence, an interesting choice given that they knew they would be watched and judged by outsiders.

'Camera!' called the director, in his best director voice. The young presenter froze. No words came. 'Cut!' called the director. I waited for the angry tirade that I knew was coming. Except that it didn't. 'Not to worry,' the director said, 'that was just a practice. Now we'll do it for real.' And they did, and it worked. I was hugely impressed by their social maturity and their professionalism. On the way back, we passed a class-room where lines of boys were bent over their desks. 'Who are they?' I asked. 'Oh, those are the clever ones,' the boys told me. 'We are the stupid guys.'

Shutting up adolescent teenagers in rows of desks when they are bubbling with energy and searching for their identity does not, on the face of it, make a lot of sense. The scope for the development of five of those seven Cs is limited in a classroom, nor should we even expect the young to take our word for it that what they learn of the first two Cs will be useful in four years' time. Perhaps our ancestors were right to allow their young people to leave that classroom at 14 and enter the world of work where they learnt the skills and self-discipline that they needed. Today, employers expect their workers to come fully formed. That is putting an unfair set of expectations on a school. Professional 'formation' involves a mix of classroom and apprenticeship, in medicine, architecture, law and accountancy. Why should it not also apply to other workers now that all work has become much more professional?

Just as we need a closer link between family and school, so do we also need a much closer link between schools and the work organisation, with work experience massively upgraded from a cursory week of watching to a mini-apprenticeship linked to their studies and certificated at 16. For many, that mini-apprenticeship could then become a full apprenticeship linked to a further education college. Germany has shown how well the apprenticeship system can work, with over 700 different schemes on offer. A university education need not be for everyone or even for most. Or it can be done later as a mature student. University is too often wasted on the young. The Sarah E. Goode STEM Academy in Chicago provides a four-year (14–18) curriculum in STEM skills (that's science, technology, engineering and maths) with every graduating student guaranteed a job with the school's corporate partner, IBM, who has helped to design the curriculum. There are 29 such academies due to open in two US states over the coming years. Britain currently has 30 similar colleges, the UTCs (university technical colleges), with 26 more planned. A further cluster of 'career colleges' is starting up, preparing 14- to 18-year-olds for careers in hospitality, digital arts or catering. This type of partnership offers both the motivation to learn and the relevant skills to enter work, often with the promise of a job on successful completion. That is learning with a point.

There is also the option of self-study through distance learning or the new MOOCs (massive open online courses), free courses offered by leading universities through the internet, although with drop-out rates of 95 per cent these are unlikely to ever be more than an accessory to more serious courses. Those three or four years away at university have become a rite of passage for one-half of a generation before entering the world of work, but for many it is an increasingly expensive way of filling in time with too few faculty staff these days to provide the kind of individual attention that I received. It seems very likely that these expensive residential undergraduate degrees will become much shorter, with more studying done by distance learning, leaving universities to concentrate on postgraduate studies and professional qualifications, with any pre-requirements tested by entrance examinations and interviews.

A better alternative would be an extension of the modular degree, or what is being called 'competence-based education', in which students take modules as and when they want or need to, often combining their academic study with practical work, a sort of self-organised apprenticeship programme, but one designed for lifelong learning. In the USA the Southern New Hampshire University College of America is offering competence-based degrees for only $2,500 a year. Other colleges are beginning to follow suit.

That would also make it easier for older students to re-enter education at any level and to earn while they learn. The idea is not new. My wife left school at 16 with no grades worth having, but three Open University courses qualified her for a part-time degree programme which she combined with her ongoing work as a photographer. It took her five years on and off. She eventually graduated at age 50, on the same day that our son got his degree after a conventional university course. Arguably she got more from her degree than he did from his, although he undoubtedly got huge enjoyment from the rite of passage.

When young people are maturing earlier it seems odd that we are steadily postponing the entry into serious work, asking for ever more evidence of scholastic achievement before paying anyone a wage. Better surely to pay them to learn while they work at every level, fitting in the university or college learning when it is appropriate. It would be a good investment for the employer and for the country. Organisations need to live up to their responsibilities as the real schools for work, just as, at the other end, families need to shoulder theirs as the schools for life, with formal education as the linking bridge. Together they would create a Second Curve that would benefit everyone.

It would pay the government to foster such initiatives by subsidies or by tax relief on apprenticeships and even on course fees for individuals, offset by savings on undergraduate universities. To pay for all this we should reconsider an education tax, not confined to university graduates but to all post-school development, paid after completion and scaled according to the cost of the particular process. If education truly provides increased earning power then it only seems just that a proportion of that extra money should be paid back to the state through taxation, leaving the original courses to be free at the point of entry.

Education is expensive. When so much of it seems to be wasted it is time for a rethink, for a Second Curve, before it is too late.

14

THE CHALLENGES OF
DEMOCRACY

Is it fit for purpose?

A GOVERNMENT OF all the people, by all the people,
for all the people was Theodore Parker's famous definition of democracy back in 1850. He called it his idea
of freedom. That seems a distant dream today when
murmurings of discontent are everywhere to be heard,
and not only in Britain. Trust in governments and
politicians has evaporated in recent times, destroying
the harmony of the nation. What has gone wrong?

There are, in my view, three reasons for this discontent in Britain: the dangerous seduction of history, the
combination rather than the separation of powers, and
the failure to move to a proper devolved or federal
system. The result, to an outsider, appears to be a
fossilised system, run by a closed circle in an overly
centralised structure. Because Britain had muddled
along more or less successfully for centuries it had
reached the top of the first curve and saw little reason
to change. The Scottish referendum in the autumn of

2014 was a belated wake-up call that should lead to a Second Curve before it is too late.

The seduction of history is well illustrated at the very heart of the British government, in the Houses of Parliament. In 1547 King Edward VI, a Protestant king, gave Parliament the use of St Stephen's Chapel in the Palace of Westminster to use as their debating chamber since the chapel would no longer have a religious use. The chapel had two rows of stalls facing each other, a screen at one end with two double doors and a raised platform for the altar with a crucifix above it. It only held 300 people, so could only hold two-thirds of the members. The members made the best use of it that they could. They used the double doors as a voting device, requiring those in favour of a proposal to walk through one door and those against through the other. They propped up their speaker on the altar platform and required the members to bow to the crucifix as they entered or left the chamber.

The chapel was destroyed by fire in 1834, rebuilt and then destroyed again by bombs in the Second World War. On both occasions it was decided to rebuild it in the same format with two opposing rows, and, again, too small to accommodate more than two-thirds of the members. Still, to this day, MPs vote by walking through those two doors, they still bow on entering or leaving although the crucifix is no longer there, there is still no room for them all to sit and they still line up on opposing benches, making it more difficult, psychologically, to find common cause. So it is that the expedient use of an unneeded chapel 450 years ago still shapes the way our laws are debated and decided. Only in Britain does history have such power. Churchill said at the time of the second rebuild, 'We shape our buildings, and afterwards our buildings shape us.' He could have substituted the word 'history' for buildings with equal justification.

There is often a whiff of romance in history and there are those who would maintain that there is a certain logic in this particular history, that an intimate chamber encourages debate, that opposing benches suggest a two-party system which many feel produces stronger government, and that you need good reason to change the status quo even if that status was the result of a chance expediency so long ago. But history can be the enemy of innovation and nostalgia leads as often as not to Davy's Bar, ignoring or not noticing a better route to the future, a Second Curve.

Since we now have elected parliamentarians who are meant to be working full-time it is only sensible to provide space for them all to attend debates without the excuse that there may not be a seat. Moreover, now that the two-party system is evolving into coalition government in every country, including Britain, a horseshoe chamber would more realistically represent the new reality and reduce the adversarial nature of the debates in favour of more consensus. More generally, an adversarial process in which one side wins is not necessarily or often the best way to arrive at the right solution or the truth, be it in policymaking or in the law courts. A senior judge told me of his relief when becoming a judge and leaving his role as a barrister. 'Now,' he said, 'I can really search for the truth. As a barrister it was my duty to work for my client, irrespective of guilt or innocence. I found that hard.'

In Parliament, as in most of life, compromise is usually the best way forward, but compromise is hard to find when the situation is defined as us against you and when history and the buildings reinforce it. In the United States compromise was assumed by the founding fathers of the constitution. The doctrine of the separation of powers was also seen as a balance of powers, working together for the good of the country. Make the process adversarial and the system freezes up, as happened to the Obama administration.

We need to question the relevance of history in other aspects of government as well as the House of Commons. Take, for instance, the dilemma facing a British prime minister on the first day in office. The first requirement is to form an executive team to run the country, helped of course by a well-established and sophisticated Civil Service. A government is allowed by statute only 84 paid ministers who have to be drawn from members of Parliament, mainly from the elected members of the House of Commons. If the election went well there might be a pool of some 400 to choose from. These individuals, however, were not originally elected for their record as managers or leaders, nor expected by anyone to have the competences required to run a state department. Any CEO of a multinational business, faced with such a limited pool of talent, would call in the executive search agencies immediately. On reflection it is amazing that the country works as well as it does, but it could be accused of being a closed shop, something that it deplores in other areas of life.

Could it be different? I was alerted by Professor Anthony King to the surprising fact that Britain and Ireland are the only countries out of the 28 members of the European Union who deem it necessary to draw all their ministers from their parliaments. In all the other countries ministers either must not be members of the parliament, or may be but do not have to be. One way round the British problem has been to recruit outsiders with the requisite experience and introduce them to Parliament through the House of Lords. Gordon Brown tried this with his 'goats' (Government of All the Talents) only to find, as others had done before him, that the new recruits found the parliamentary system too stifling, even in the gentlemanly atmosphere of the Lords, and soon departed.

Why then, one has to ask, does Britain have to be so different, so deferential to tradition? Even Walter Bagehot, the recognised authority on the (unwritten) British constitution, puts it this way: 'The Cabinet . . . is a board of control chosen by the legislature, out of persons whom it trusts and knows, to rule the country. The particular mode in which the English ministers are selected . . . the rule which limits the choice of the Cabinet to the members of the legislature – are accidents incidental to its definition . . . A cabinet which included persons not members of the legislative assembly might still perform all useful duties.'

The British have, in the past, felt it right to combine the three roles of government, the legislature, the executive and the judiciary, in one assembly, albeit in two Houses. It was intended to produce more harmony and consistency. Too much so, one might suspect, because that is exactly what a dictatorship does: it combines the three roles. Indeed, the British have sometimes been accused of having an elected dictatorship, given that, before the days of coalitions, once elected with a decent majority the executive had untrammelled power. Recently, the British have separated out the judiciary into a stand-alone Supreme Court. Maybe they should do the same with the executive, still holding it accountable to Parliament, still bound by its legislation, but no longer belonging to it. The accountability would be enforced through the Select Committee system rather than the hothouse of the House of Commons. It would be no different from the USA, or the Netherlands, or Denmark, or many others. François Hollande, when he became President of France, at first promised to appoint only elected persons to his cabinet but soon had to go back on his promise when he needed to appoint a banker to be his new minister for the economy.

As it stands, the system is confusing. Ministers have to give time and attention to the constituencies who elected them as well as to their ministerial responsibilities. These are often at odds with each other and leave too little time for either. More worrying is the reality that anyone aspiring to help run the country needs first to be elected to Parliament. The result is that politics has become a career, often starting with work in a think tank or a party political office, followed by a dutiful adherence to party discipline. The same applies to the Civil Service in Britain: the best start early, right after college. The result can be that the country ends up being run by people with little experience of the world beyond politics or of management and excludes those who do not wish to commit themselves to a career so early in their lives or who value their independence. Were more ministers and secretaries of state to be drawn from outside the political circles, there might be a better chance of their departments taking a longer-term view, less concerned about the implications for their re-election or promotion. No doubt it would change gradually, with the main offices of state continuing to be filled by members of the legislature, but with the precedent once established the practice might grow.

The longer-term view might also be reinforced if there were to be an independent statutory body responsible for the maintenance and development of the infrastructure of the country, not one that was part of the Treasury, as at present in the UK. New Zealand has recently enlarged the role of its Civil Service Commissioner to include a responsibility for stewardship. It is, perhaps deliberately, an ill-defined term but one that might well include an oversight of the longer-term infrastructure. Another alternative would be to make it the responsibility of a reformed and much smaller House of Lords, recreated as a Senate with a College of Senators appointed for fixed terms of, say, 15 years, experts in their fields and without the anachronistic embellishment of titles. They would be there not only to act as a revising chamber for new legislation, as at present, but also to be the guardian of the long-term future. Were Britain one day to begin to build up a reserve fund for major investments this then could be the responsibility of the new Senate. It would give the Senate a more active role in the future of the state in addition to its auditing or checking responsibilities.

If Britain were to entertain such a notion and start a Second Curve she might have to break with another tradition and move to a formal constitution that cements the agreed areas of responsibilities in law. We might also celebrate the 800th anniversary of the Magna Carta by updating this, our only semblance of a formal constitution. A formal legal constitution would help to deal with the next source of confusion for both government and work organisations, the problem of managing internal differences. Every country has bits that are prosperous alongside areas of deprivation, teeming cities and emptying villages. Economically it makes sense to treat everything and everywhere the same but, although the economies of scale are clear, everything is not the same everywhere. Incalculable, too, is the sense of grievance felt by those who can feel ignored, disenfranchised and demotivated. London is another country, they say in the north of Britain, but looking at it the other way round, so is the north, or Cornwall, which was recently granted protected minority status by the European Union, putting it alongside the rest of the Celtic nations.

The obvious answer is federalism, a well-tried system which the British recommended to their departing colonies and dominions and defeated enemies, such as Germany, where it demonstrably works rather well, but resolutely shunned at home. Federalism is not the same as decentralisation. Although power is distributed it is granted by the parts to the centre, a form of reverse delegation that goes by the ugly name of subsidiarity. Subsidiarity is part of Catholic social teaching. It was defined by Pope Pius XI in 1931 with the words 'one should not withdraw from individuals and commit to the community what they can accomplish by their own enterprises and industry', or, in my interpretation, stealing people's choices is morally wrong. That theft is what causes so much of the murmuring in the disaffected parts of the United Kingdom and in other non-federal countries as well.

In theory, in a federal system, the parts agree to cede to the centre the responsibilities and duties that they believe that the centre can do better on their behalf than they can on their own. In practice the division of responsibilities is a matter of negotiation. If dictated by the centre alone the contract will not hold. Given more freedom to pay for and run their own affairs, the new regions will have every incentive to make the best of the resources that they have, even to compete with other parts of the federation. Federalism releases energy, encourages experiment, builds local pride and loyalty, but is still big where it counts. It combines the strength of size with local difference. What works so well in Germany might also work well in France, Spain, Italy and Britain, all countries that are struggling to hold their different parts together. Cities, and their football clubs, already engender more loyalty than the nation state, which itself is a relatively recent idea and one that is currently being pulled apart in parts of the world. Federalism, importantly, requires people to have a sense of two citizenships, to the whole and to the local. Someone can rejoice in being both Texan and American, Bavarian and German as well as European. Sovereignty, *pace* Margaret Thatcher, can be shared and perhaps should be more often, as the world looks for a variety of combinations in order to survive in a global maelstrom.

Federalism is complicated in its details, but not confusing if done properly. It looks untidy, with many anomalies which efficiency enthusiasts long to put straight, but its advantages are that it leaves the individual parts free to be different in the way that suits them. Large organisations are slowly realising that political ideas and theories often have more to tell them than management manuals. Federalism is a new curve whose time has come. Differences can no longer be ironed out or ignored. They have to be recognised and legitimised or they will boil over. As a result, large organisations, including governments, are slowly moving into muddled forms of federalism, often without calling it that or even realising it. They would find it less confusing if they followed the well-established requirements of a federal body, particularly the ideas of subsidiarity, or reverse delegation, and the separation of powers.

In any case, once agreed, the division of responsibilities would need to be recorded as a formal constitution. Britain is sliding slowly into a quasi-federation or what they prefer to call 'devo max', to avoid that dreaded f-word. The new federal Britain would include Wales, Northern Ireland, Scotland and, maybe, five English megacities or regions. Progress is complicated by the fact that it would be hard to divide up England geographically, by city or region, while England on its own would be too dominant. Surveys also reveal that while the local bureaucrats enthuse about more devolution their citizens are not so keen, preferring that the big decisions are still taken at the centre. Unusually, rather than demanding it, they might have to have autonomy thrust upon them.

A negotiated federalism always has to be a slow and tentative slide needing goodwill by all parties. Nevertheless, had a federation of Britain been in existence earlier it would have saved many confusions and much unhappiness. Confederations are different, being looser forms of federalism, where subsidiarity is much stronger and only limited areas of shared responsibility are agreed. Europe is fundamentally a confederation of nation states with specific agreements on particular areas, mainly to do with the free movement of trade, people and finance and, some say, too much else. Pushing it into a full federation would only happen if Europe as a whole felt threatened by outside forces, although a subset of nations might well set up their own federation within the larger body.

As it is, with power too centralised in many countries, representative democracy is losing its potency. Too many people do not bother to vote, either because they no longer trust their elected politicians to act honourably or competently or because they do not feel that their vote will make any difference. A federal system in which local issues were decided locally and largely paid for locally would pull in more voters who could see that their votes made a difference. It would also help if it were made easier to vote. Electronic voting via the internet must surely come one day. It is already in use in Estonia, despite warnings about the security of the system.

Already, in Britain, I must by law file my VAT

returns through the government website, but not so with my voting choice. Instead, to vote in an election, should I choose the option of postal voting I will fill in a postal voting form, giving only my date of birth and National Insurance number, put it in a complicated set of envelopes and send it off well before the election day. Why would it be different if I did it electronically, with my personal ID and password and code? Of course we would miss all the television images of the count and the night-long wait for the outcome because the results could be counted almost immediately, but we would miss, too, the late Thursday evening walk in the rain to the local school hall to put an X in a box behind a curtain, having had our name ticked off on a list by someone whose only check on us is that we are carrying what they assume is our voter registration card. How secure is that, I ask, when people suggest that electronic voting is subject to abuse.

Ritual is important. It adds significance to things. I can see that requiring MPs to vote by walking through those doors inherited from St Stephen's Chapel not only means that they have to be present and counted, in person, but also acts as a reminder of why they are there, even if they sometimes don't know what they are voting on, just following their herd. Some rituals, however, are just nostalgia and eventually become dysfunctional. Manual voting is now one of them. If we want people, particularly the young, to take democracy seriously we have to work with the new ways of communicating.

Otherwise we risk going down Clayton Christensen's technological mudslide on the road to Davy's Bar. The Scottish referendum in 2014, with an 84 per cent turnout, showed that when it matters to them the voters will come out, come rain, hail or sunshine, but not all elections are so emotive or so compelling – witness the turnout for European elections.

One unfortunate outcome of electronic voting might be an increase in popular referenda. There is an inherent conflict between representative democracy and the direct democracy of the referendum. You cannot sensibly have both. Political decisions are complex. They require careful and expert analysis. They can seldom be reduced to one simple question, leaving most of the assumptions and consequences unstated. Why not leave the responsibility to those who have been chosen precisely because they are thought competent to take such decisions on our behalf? As Edmund Burke, that great Whig politician, reminded the electors of Bristol, he was elected by them to govern the country, not to advance their local cause, to be their representative not their delegate. Although the electors disagreed and turned him out at the next election, Burke's distinction between representative and delegate is crucial to a representative democracy. Referenda would emasculate it and drain it of talent.

If people want to influence the decisions that most directly concern them they need to become active citizens in their own locality, something that federalism would make easier, although yet another change in the language that we use would help. Britain still calls its people subjects although it teaches citizenship in its schools. The language tells us something. Subjects are meant to do as they are told. Citizens are the point and the strength of a nation. They have rights, but also obligations, and are active, or should be, not passive. But if people are going to become active citizens it must be first made easier for them, they must be able to see some of the results of their vote as they appear in local differences. To become more directly involved they must also see their involvement as a chance to make a difference. At present local government in Britain is essentially a delivery agent for central government, which dictates and provides over three-quarters of their expenditure. Until this changes the role of councillor will not be thought by many to be worth sacrificing one's evenings for.

For too long it has been assumed by too many that there is little they can do to affect the way things are done. That is not a good basis for active citizenship. Government must become more open and more real to its people. That will require some major adjustments to the way the country is run and to the assumptions that underpin it. It is not too soon to plan for that Second Curve.

15

THE NECESSITY OF OTHERS

Who are they? Where do we find them?
How do we keep them?

'NO MAN IS an island', said John Donne, 'entire of itself.' We need others to allow us to feel wanted and useful, loved if possible, to be connected to the world. How lucky then are we to live in a time of super-connectivity. It was not always so. Around 1837 Rowland Hill, a distant ancestor of my wife, began to take an interest in the postal system of Great Britain. In a sense it was nothing to do with him, he was the headmaster of a visionary school for boys at Bruce Castle in Tottenham. He needed to find a way to motivate his young pupils to learn to read and it occurred to him that a reformed postal system might be the way to do it. At that time letters were rare and expensive – one shilling and sixpence to go from London to Edinburgh – and postage was paid by the recipient on arrival. Only the rich wrote home, and only then if they were sure that there was someone there who was prepared to pay to hear from them. Families lost touch with sons and daughters who had moved far away, romances languished when couples had to move apart, as Hill discovered after he came across a young woman distressed because she could not afford to pay for a letter sent to her by her fiancé. Out of sight was, too often, out of mind.

Rowland Hill set out to reconnect the nation and, incidentally, to provide a reason for his boys to learn to read and write. He had the revolutionary idea of pricing all letters at one penny, no matter how far they had to travel, and reversed the payment process by requiring them to be pre-franked, eventually with a separate stamp which could be bought in advance, the original penny black. The scheme was mocked for its impracticality and Hill for his impertinence for dabbling in matters beyond his concern. Such is the lot of all visionaries. But good sense prevailed and in 1839 the postal system was altered and Hill put in charge. Within a few years the penny post idea had been copied around the world. Rowland Hill had reconnected the world, not just the nation. It was a Second Curve, brought about by just one individual.

In a sense, Tim Berners-Lee, another Englishman, was Rowland Hill reborn 150 years later, for the internet and its offspring, the social media, have connected the world in a miraculous and wonderful way which we now take for granted. But being connected does not necessarily mean being close. Having 20,000 followers on Twitter does not equal having 20,000 contacts, let alone 20,000 friends. When a friend boasted that he had received birthday greetings from 120 friends I asked him if he knew them all. 'I must have met them some-time, somewhere,' he said. 'Or your iPhone did, you mean,' I replied. You can be lonely in a crowd, as I know only too well, but, conversely, you can also be alone and comfortable in a room by yourself. Alone and lonely are very different.

There is growing evidence, too, that too much communication can be bad for you. Facebook encour-ages some to project fantasies of themselves that they cannot then live up to. When all around you are twit-tering away and broadcasting their achievements it is easy to feel that you are missing out, even that you are a failure. It is as easy to feel the stranger in the room in social media as at a noisy party. Loneliness isn't solved by having an iPhone in your pocket. It can even make it worse. I watch people on the Tube or in buses compulsively checking their messages again and again, hoping to find another one waiting for them. Loneliness can just be an empty inbox on your phone.

Loneliness, of one sort or another, has come to be the new poverty in modern society. The British, it seems, are particularly lonely, the second loneliest in Europe after the Germans. Only 58 per cent feel connected to people in their locality. One in eight of them has no one to call on and says that the TV or a pet is their best friend. Half of all people over 75 live alone and about one million in Britain say they often go for a month without speaking to anyone, apart from routine encounters at the checkout. The research findings on the consequences of loneliness should alarm us all: loneliness, it seems, increases the risk of cognitive decline, dementia, high blood pressure, heart disease and depression. It is more dangerous to your health to be lonely than to be obese, being equivalent to smoking 15 cigarettes a day. All this is despite the array of new ways to connect with each other, the volunteer befriending schemes and specialist housing for the elderly.

Loneliness, however, I would suggest, is nothing to do with the number of names in your address book, nor is it to do with propinquity or connectivity. It is, instead, the feeling of your not mattering much to anyone, of going unnoticed in the world. Unfortunately you won't matter to anyone else if they do not matter to you. You cannot expect your neighbours to call you if you never call them; it's no good castigating your children for neglecting you if you always take from them and never give. Mattering has to be reciprocal. This mutual concern is always easier if individuals are connected by some joint endeavour, be it work, child-rearing, home, sport or community activity. Loneliness is on the increase because more and more people now have to live and work as loners. There is often too little that is pulling them together, doing things that require a joint commitment. Even sharing a common space can help. One downside of the self-responsible society is a lack of that joint endeavour or even of a common meeting place. Without these no amount of Facebook messages will make any difference.

That is why the workplace is so socially important, even if the work itself is boring or seems pointless. It is a personal connecting zone. There is no need to pity the old codger at the checkout, he is there for the tea breaks and the chats as much as for the money. It is why families have always been a linchpin of society even when they bicker among themselves, why churches, synagogues, mosques and temples have long been valued as places of togetherness. It matters not how quarrelsome some families can be, or how disputatious the religious gathering, or how loud some of the other customers are. At least, for a time, you are one of them. You are not an island.

For some the gym has replaced the church or the office as a social space. For others it is the local Starbucks or Costa coffee shop, the hairdresser's, nail bar or betting shop, what I think of as chatty outlets that link people into a community of like-minded folk. Local bookstores are evolving into chatty outlets with their own coffee corners. Libraries and supermarkets could follow their example and create chatty corners. We need more social spaces, argues Katharine Whitehorn, places where we can go as of right, preferably without paying too much or for free, where it is socially acceptable to speak to others without introduction.

You would, however, do better still if you were linked to another personal island or to a group of similar islands. Friendship is a case of mutual mattering, to be treasured and nurtured. It breaks down if it only works one way. Marriage, or its equivalent, is friendship at its most intimate while families are still the most universal of social groupings, even the modern flexi-families with steps and halves and the occasional ex included in the mix. Not long ago I was talking about my daughter when one of those listening said, 'Does your wife have a daughter too?' I saw then that two sets of children, his and hers, were more common than I had realised, but also that I must always talk of 'our' daughter in future.

Families, however, are a problem as well as an obvious opportunity for that elusive supportive together-ness. They should be better than any coffee shop as a place of mutual support, ready-made as they are at birth as a place of shared destiny. Sadly, of course, no one chooses the family they were born into nor even the one that comes with the person you marry. It is not guaranteed that your brother or sister, mother or father will be a kindred spirit. The story of Cain and Abel has resonated down the centuries as an example of sibling jealousy, although not all end in fratricide as that one did. I have often sympathised with the elder brother in the parable of the prodigal son, who had to witness the affection and generosity lavished on his erring brother while his own faithful service was taken for granted. Families are not always models of harmony.

Nevertheless there is a shared history in every family

and an implied obligation because of that. When all else fails, the family – or part of it – will still be there, even if silently resentful. There are around 6 million family carers in Britain, mostly unpaid, working for love or, maybe, reluctant obligation. Families are nature's breakdown service as well as its pool of residual love. They are worth the maintenance effort, if only because you may need them one day. Family gatherings on key occasions, good communication with those out of earshot, telephone and Skype calls and even family websites to share good news and bad, these are all well-established ways of sustaining that sense of belonging that makes a family something more than a piece of personal history.

Families are growing bigger. I knew only one of my grandparents and she died when I was 9 years old. Our children knew every one of their grandparents and many now have living great-grandparents as well, let alone step-grandparents and a wealth of cousins of different generations. With such a variety of relation-ships, families should more correctly be called tribes. It may be easier for some to think of themselves as belonging to a tribe rather than a family. There is more room to pick and choose whom you feel closer to, less pressure to conform, more space for individual differ-ence. If, as I often think, a change in the words we use heralds a change in practice, then substituting tribe for family will signal a rethinking about our families and the relationship between their members.

Perhaps we need a new word for marriage as well, to reflect the new flexibility of that institution. Marriage is too loaded with religious overtones for some, and partnership sounds too weak, too unemotional. I do not have the solution, only the observation that our difficulty with the language is a symptom of our changing society. A formal and legal commitment does, however, seem to make a difference to the younger members. A study of 15-year-old teenagers in Britain unearthed the fact that only three in ten of them were living in a home with two parents if those parents had originally been cohabiting, whereas seven out of ten were still living with two parents if those were formally married. Maybe the politicians are right, the legal commitment involved in a marriage is the best foundation for a family, at least in the early years, although to think that a small tax advantage would make a difference seems a bit insulting.

Marriages of any sort are now no longer expected, by many, to last for life. Prenuptial agreements are becoming more common and divorce an accepted event. In Victorian times the average marriage lasted 15 years, much the same as today. The difference is that Victorian marriages, and those of even earlier days, ended when one partner, usually the wife, died. Now they end because of divorce or separation. Perhaps 15 to 20 years is a more natural length for a relationship, with the option to renew. My wife and I have been married for 52 years – and we still regard each other as our one best friend. So a long committed relationship is possible, but we explicitly changed our implicit marriage contract halfway through. For the first 25 years I was the absent weekday husband, earning the money, while my wife ran the home, raised the children and helped out financially with a part-time business. Our daytime lives were separate and so were many of our friendship networks. When the children left home and I became self-employed our lives changed. My wife resumed her photography career but also became my literary agent and manager. We worked together on my projects and hers, combining our skills and splitting the cooking and housekeeping. Now we share everything. There is no one that I know whom she does not also know, and vice versa. While other men sometimes exchange their wife for a colleague at work, we did it the other way round: my wife became my colleague and that rekindled our relationship. I often say, only partly in jest, that like many others we meet, I am on my second marriage – but to the same woman.

All relationships need refreshing from time to time, particularly the close ones. People change, circumstances change. To terminate the relationship may be too drastic, too distressing to others who may be affected. Better, as a first step anyway, to explore a new contract. Thinking of the relationship as a contract, an exchange of expectations, may sound too formal, too legalistic, too unromantic if it is a marriage, but in a time when people no longer want to be bound by tradition, when they need the freedom to define themselves in new ways, it can be useful to explore the possibilities of a different way of being together.

Love, at its best, matures into a deep friendship, friendship which is the best remedy for feelings of isolation, inadequacy or hopelessness, the best opportunity, too, for rejoicing in togetherness, for sharing bad times as well as good. Francis Bacon, the 16th-century English philosopher and essayist, ended an essay on friendship saying: 'A man cannot speak to his son but as a father; to his wife but as a husband; to his enemy but upon terms; whereas a friend may speak as the case requires . . . if [a man] have not a friend he may quit the stage.' There are friends and friends, some whom it is good to party with or sport with, but fewer on whom you could rely to run to your aid when needed or to speak truth to your face in the Bacon way. It is wise to grapple those few to yourself with hoops of steel because they are valuable beyond measure. Facebook 'friends', unfortunately, don't seem to count. Most of the young when surveyed felt that there was no one among their 'friends' whom they could count on in an emergency. The new e-communities of mutual interest are also fragile, not to be relied upon for more than sharing.

Now in my eighties, I find that old and trusted friends are especially precious, and getting fewer as more come to the end of their days. New friends, when they happen, are exciting, but until one has shared some deep experience together they are unlikely to be part of that small group of trusties. As one ages the friendship network inevitably shrinks. I felt for a friend in his nineties who lamented that all his contemporaries were gone and that the young, quite clearly, felt only sympathy for him, not true friendship. I resolved then that in some way or other, it was imperative that I should remain interesting to the generation below me, be it by wit or wisdom, occasionally seasoned with some judicious generosity. Life without others to share it with is akin to watching the grass grow: boring, lonely and meaningless.

Remaining interesting to, and interested in, others is the principal challenge of old age. The sequence should best be the other way round, for unless we are clearly interested in others they won't be very interested in us. It is tempting when old to talk too much, tell the familiar stories once again, proffer advice when it has not been requested. Better by far to learn first from those others, particularly the younger ones, to enter their world before inviting them into yours, as long as your curiosity is genuine. The rewards can be huge, for the young are the future and the future has to be more interesting than the past that we know too well. To glimpse the world as they see it can be a privilege. To stay connected, however, one has to use their means of connectivity, which means getting to grips with the social media and the new technologies.

In a book such as this, primarily addressed to those

starting out in life, I would plead with the young to cultivate their elders. There is often silliness there but also wisdom and much experience. The world may seem to have changed a lot in the last 70 years, let alone the last thousand, but much remains the same. History may not repeat itself but it has its lessons, lessons that the old know better because they have had to learn them too. Societies that shut away their elders are wasting a precious resource.

Overall, the new variety of relationships makes the choice of friends or significant others much wider, but it also means that no firm relationships come ready-made. Your friendship circle is not restricted to your colleagues at work or the family you grew up with, but that also means that they have less of an obligation to you. More than ever before, in spite of and because of the greater choice, we are on our own. But if John Donne was right we cannot survive on our own. We all need others and to have them they must also need us. If we are to ride the new curves of society in any comfort we will need the support of others, good friends wherever we can find them. Loneliness kills.

16

THE CONTRACT WITH
OURSELVES

What do we want from life?

IN THE END it all comes down to the perennial question, 'What is it all for?' Why do we so strive so earnestly to improve our lot and that of society? What does improvement mean anyway, or success for that matter? Having put society to rights in these essays we need to stand back and ask, 'Why? What then?' And where better to start than with Gandhi. The old sage was right, surely, when he said that we have to be the change we want to see. Pontificating about a better society is easy, but to make it happen it has to start with us, with what we see as our own sequence of curves in life. What are we prepared to do or to contribute in order to get where? In short, what is our contract with ourselves?

It were well, then, if we knew what kind of person we would like to be, what sort of life we wanted to live, what values we should live by. That is not easy when you are starting out, when life stretches out before you like an open plain empty of any landmarks. Nor will it be enough to declare, as I once did, that we want to make the world a better place. First we need to define what better would mean instead of rushing blindly into the fray. I was as guilty as anyone in my eagerness to get going, to anywhere as long as it wasn't here, where I was.

I once described my life to an Indian guru. He listened politely to the extended list of my activities, then said, 'You seem to be very busy going nowhere in particular.' He was right, I realised. My life had no direction. I had never addressed the big question: 'What am I here for?' If you don't know your destination life can be just random travelling, the direction chosen by your travelling companions or by temporary impulse. I was like that once. I remember sitting in the living room of our home in Ireland with my rather bemused parents, thumbing through a pile of recruitment brochures from businesses in distant parts of the world. I was looking for a job. All I knew was that I didn't want to stay in Ireland or Britain. I wanted to see the world and earn a good living while I did so. I was treating my life as if it were a holiday to be decided by the allure of the brochures. I was lucky. There were jobs aplenty in those days. I could choose but would have chosen better if I had the right criteria, and if I had remembered Aristotle.

As I mentioned earlier, I ended up in South-East Asia working for an oil company, much to the dismay of my parents who, I suspect, imagined me running a Chinese petrol station. It gave me, I must admit, a few enjoyable years in the sun and the heat but I eventually realised that it was not what I wanted, that to continue would be a waste of my life. So, before jumping into the next experience, I needed to work out what sort of life I wanted and what I could contribute with it. It was then that I also read a lovely book, *A Pattern of Islands*, the autobiography of a British colonial officer in the South Pacific, Sir Arthur Grimble. He told how he had pursued his chosen career because he wanted to impress his uncles, only to wake up one day and realise that they were all dead. Without meaning to, uncles, aunts and parents can get in the way of our life choices. Jean-Paul Sartre once said that the best gift that a father can give his children is to die young. I told mine that I had no plans to be so generous, but that I hoped they would not feel the need to justify their lives to me or to their mother, because that would just be another way of postponing the quest for the real purpose of their life.

As it was I spent the first five decades of my life trying to be someone that I thought I should be but wasn't. It wasn't until my fifties that I became comfortable in my own skin. I don't, however, regret those lost decades because I probably needed to try out other identities before I found the right one. I only wish that the decades had been shorter. We should, I conclude, never be afraid of trying on a new identity. Indeed I often say to those starting out that your twenties are an excellent time to experiment, as long as you don't do any harm to anyone. It is always useful to discover what you don't want to be so that you can at least cross that one off the list and move on.

Only when you know who you want to be can you settle on what you want out of life. Many in our capitalist age would settle for money, and then more money, as the answer. That would translate as profit in the case of a business and economic growth for a country. Money keeps the options open. Which only postpones the problem, for money is only an intermediate purpose, a means to a bigger end. It cannot logically be an end in itself because it is only a token of exchange, so you have to ask what it is buying. One thing is clear, that after a certain level, seemingly around £15,000 income per year, more money does not buy happiness, for there are always others with even more money to keep you wanting more. Recently I came across the diary I had kept for a while at school. At age 17 I had written that all I wanted in life was £2,000 a year and a Bentley Continental. I wasn't being all that modest: £2,000 was four times the starting salary for graduates so I was dreaming of today's equivalent of £100,000 plus car. I am ashamed now to think that I had no idea of how I was going to earn that money or how I wanted to live, other than driving around in an absurd car, but I was no different from some of the young people I come across today – money as the presumed answer to life.

The trouble is that money remains the one thing of which, it seems, you can never have enough, as the escalating (and surely unnecessary) rewards of senior executives seem to prove. Even when you have met all your needs and wants there are always the Veblen goods, so called after Thorstein Veblen's theory of comparative goods, those aspects of conspicuous expenditure that are effectively rationed, like the membership of elite clubs, the ownership of property in an exclusive zone, or being in the top ten of some league table of corporate pay. Money is also, for some, a scorecard, unrelated to anything it can buy except a place on the Forbes List of billionaires. Asked why he needed his £2 million salary, one executive agreed that he had no need for so much, that he would not work harder if offered more, or less hard if the pay was smaller, 'but others are getting it so why shouldn't I?' There can be no end to such a financial journey. It is one that must, ultimately, deliver little except the chance to pat oneself on the back. It would be nice to think that there was a greater final purpose to justify all that effort. Money, they say, is like manure, it needs to be spread around and smells if left unused in a pile. Philanthropists should therefore take a bow for turning their wealth into fertiliser but many more are needed to drown out the smell of too much money in the hands of too few people.

Settling for an intermediate goal such as money is much easier than answering the really big question,

'What is life for?' What is it all about? Governments focus on economic growth, the necessary condition, as they see it, to a better society, but one that allows them to postpone that bigger question of what such a society might look like. My business school students would focus on their next job on graduating and their immediate earning potential. Questioned about what they ultimately wanted to do with their life, they often replied, as I had, 'I'll build up some capital first and get round to that question when I'm comfortably rich.' Too often, that day never came. There was always more to be earned before they had enough. The same is true of businesses and governments. More always seems better because it offers more choices.

It is all too easy to postpone the answer to the big question, to be sidetracked by short-term attractions or requirements, in public life as much as in private, to be busy going nowhere. Democracy itself is prone to focus-group pressures as political parties manoeuvre to get elected, pandering to what they think are the popular priorities, reminding one of the Irishman who said, 'I'm your leader and I'm right behind you.' We look in vain most of the time for a political leader who is prepared to state up front what his or her vision is for society, one that goes beyond cosy platitudes about prosperity and fairness. None of them want to offer hostages to fortune in case they might have to deliver or, worse, fail to win the power to deliver. So they twist and tweak, get distracted by their little local difficulties, complain of unknown unknowns and the impossibility of pleasing everyone. Survival not progress is what most settle for in the end, to get elected, or re-elected as the case may be. Ask them why we should vote for them and they reply with a list of policies and programmes but shy away from the big questions: 'To what aim? To build what sort of society?'

Maybe we have become disillusioned with Utopia, Thomas More's word for his ideal society, which was, in truth, a rather grim place, with everyone dressing the same and sharing their wives and children. Religions claim to offer help, although by locating the ultimate goal in another world, their definition of the end purpose of life is hard to pin down. You have to have faith in their god or gods to follow their prescriptions. St Augustine's City of God was set in some other-worldly place while Plato's Republic was to be ruled by philosophers with everyone else supposed to be content with that part of society to which they were assigned. Was he serious, I sometimes wonder, or just speculating?

The hope must be that we, as individuals, will do better, that we may find some criterion against which to measure our life and decide its purpose. Two and a half millennia ago, Aristotle turned his mind to it, as he did to most other aspects of life and nature. He proceeded logically, weeding out all those intermediate goals, looking for something that was not a means to something else but had to stand alone, valuable for its own sake. He decided, in the end, that the ultimate purpose of human life was to achieve excellence in accord with virtue through eudaimonia. This he called the good life. Eudaimonia is a complex Greek word. It has usually been translated as happiness, but Aristotle did not mean a state of pleasure or contentment. He meant something much more active and productive, something more akin to Mihaly Csikszentmihalyi's idea of 'flow' or what some athletes call being 'in the zone'. I translate it as 'doing your best at what you are best at, for the benefit of others': living up to your potential, in other words. The 'benefit of others' is important because Aristotle is clear that fulfilling your potential must be done in accordance with virtue, ethically not selfishly. Man, he famously said, is a political (meaning social) animal, he is not meant to live alone. We all need a purpose beyond ourselves to feel that we have made a contribution, made a difference to someone somewhere.

Aristotle, however, was a man of his time and class. True fulfilment, he believed, could best be realised by people like himself, middle-aged, property-owning males. Intellectual contemplation was for him the most worthwhile activity. You get the feeling that, for Aristotle, life's perfection would be best achieved by reading and reflecting on a book under the shade of a tree in the afternoon, followed by a discussion of it over a good meal with friends, no doubt cooked by his wife and served by his slaves. Alasdair MacIntyre, a contemporary philosopher, described Aristotle as 'almost an English gentleman' and dismissed his idea of happiness as 'appalling'. We do not have to agree with Aristotle on his very personal interpretation of eudaimonia, but can still keep to the underlying idea that the fulfilment of one's potential should be the life goal of every one of us, as long as it was directed at the human good.

I have argued in another book that there is something that I call 'proper selfishness', that to feel successful you have first to invest in yourself but must then turn that investment to be of benefit beyond yourself in some way. If you don't first develop your own potential your contribution will be of little value. If you keep the fruits of your development to yourself it will be improper selfishness and ultimately unrewarding. I keep a white stone on my desk. It is there because of a verse in the book of Revelation in the Bible which says, 'To the one who overcomes, the angel said, I will give a white stone on which is written a new name that no one knows except the one who receives it.' The book of Revelation is one of the darkest and most mysterious books of the Bible so I cannot be sure what the message behind it is meant to imply. But I interpret it to mean that if I live up to my full potential and use it for the benefit of people beyond myself, then I will earn my new name and will, the book goes on to say, stand as one of the pillars of the temple of God, that is of society. The white stone sits there as my personal challenge to find eudaimonia and my new name, even if it takes me the rest of my life.

Aristotle, as we have noted, was a member of the leisured class in Ancient Greece. He did not have to struggle for the necessities of life. Most of us have to provide for our own economic and social needs before we are ready to concentrate on fulfilling our real potential. The pursuit of personal eudaimonia is a Second- or even Third-Curve cause, best done when you know who you are, what you can and can't do, when you are no longer consumed by the need to survive and provide. Abraham Maslow, the American psychologist, used his idea of a hierarchy of needs to suggest that it is only when you have satisfied your economic and status needs that you are ready to proceed to what he called self-actualisation, a state not dissimilar to eudaimonia. So, yes, you do need money at the outset, but it does not stop there.

Robert Skidelsky and his son Edward, in their intriguing book *How Much is Enough?*, spell out what they see as the seven necessary conditions for a good life in Aristotelian terms: health, security, respect, personality, harmony with nature, friendship, leisure. By personality they mean the freedom to develop one's own character. Leisure, the Skidelskys emphasise, need not mean no work, as long as it is work of your own choice, not toil. We can argue with their list and its definitions. The point, however, is that a good society should aim to provide these conditions so that every citizen has the opportunity to achieve a good life and personal eudaimonia.

Thomas Jefferson was an Aristotelian; his annotated Latin edition of Aristotle's works can be seen in the Library of Congress in Washington. When he promised, in the original draft of the Declaration of Independence, that every man should have the inalienable right to 'the preservation of life, and liberty, and the pursuit of happiness' he was using Aristotle's terms. He meant, I believe, that government should guarantee its people the conditions that would allow each of them to develop their full potential. The times being what they were, the Declaration did not include women or slaves. They were to follow later, much later. You could see it as a more succinct summary of the Skidelsky list.

I would go further. I would argue that it is not a bad summary of the responsibility of an organisation towards its members, one that, if properly applied, would also help it to fulfil its obligations to the other stakeholders. Any list of desiderata by employees has at its head the opportunity to develop new competences, to have the chance to grow and to enjoy more control over their own work, to make more of a contribution. We are all modern Aristotelians at heart, if only we are given the chance. If the opportunity is not granted to us we should seize it.

As a classroom exercise I have on occasion asked mature students to do the obituary exercise. 'Imagine,' I tell them, 'that you die in your mid-eighties. Your funeral is well attended and your best friend has agreed in advance to give the eulogy, but you asked him to keep it short. Write what you would like him to say in less than 300 words.' In effect I am asking people who are often at the high point of their careers, in their forties, to stand at the end of their life and look back. Their work CVs have long since been filed away or thrown in the dustbin. They have gone on to other things. What do they want to be remembered for? What will have been their most important contribution to life? What will they leave behind them? It is a sobering exercise, as I found when I first did it myself, but it also gives one permission to dream. It is intended to help the participants to put their current work and lives in perspective and to focus on any unfulfilled potential. I suspect that Aristotle would have approved because it is an exercise in contemplation, something he regarded as essential to an examined life.

The obituary exercise reminds one of the advice given by Solon, the Athenian sage and lawgiver, to King Croesus, who was looking to be congratulated on his riches, success and happiness: 'Call no man happy until the end be known.' Too true, as it turned out, since Croesus subsequently lost everything including his kingdom and ended up in chains on top of a funeral pyre. Even when you think you have done enough you have not, for there is always more, until the end. To rest risks unhappiness, with no work, no hope and worst of all, perhaps, no one to love. Frederick

Wiseman is 84; he showed his latest documentary in Cannes in 2014. Asked why he goes on making films he said, 'All my friends are either dead or still working.' There is always work to be done, a Second Curve waiting to be invented.